This Coloring Book Belongs To:

Color Chart

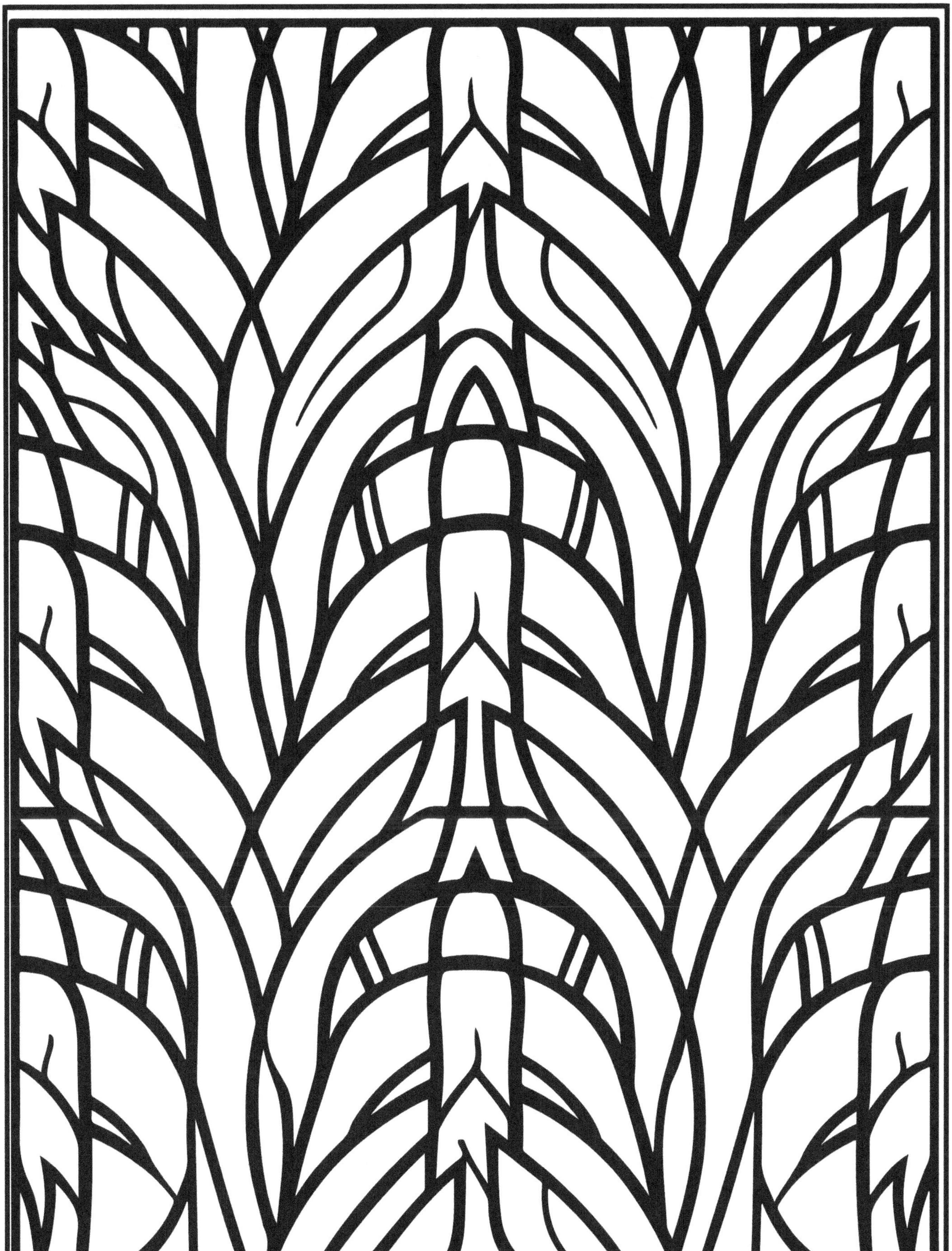

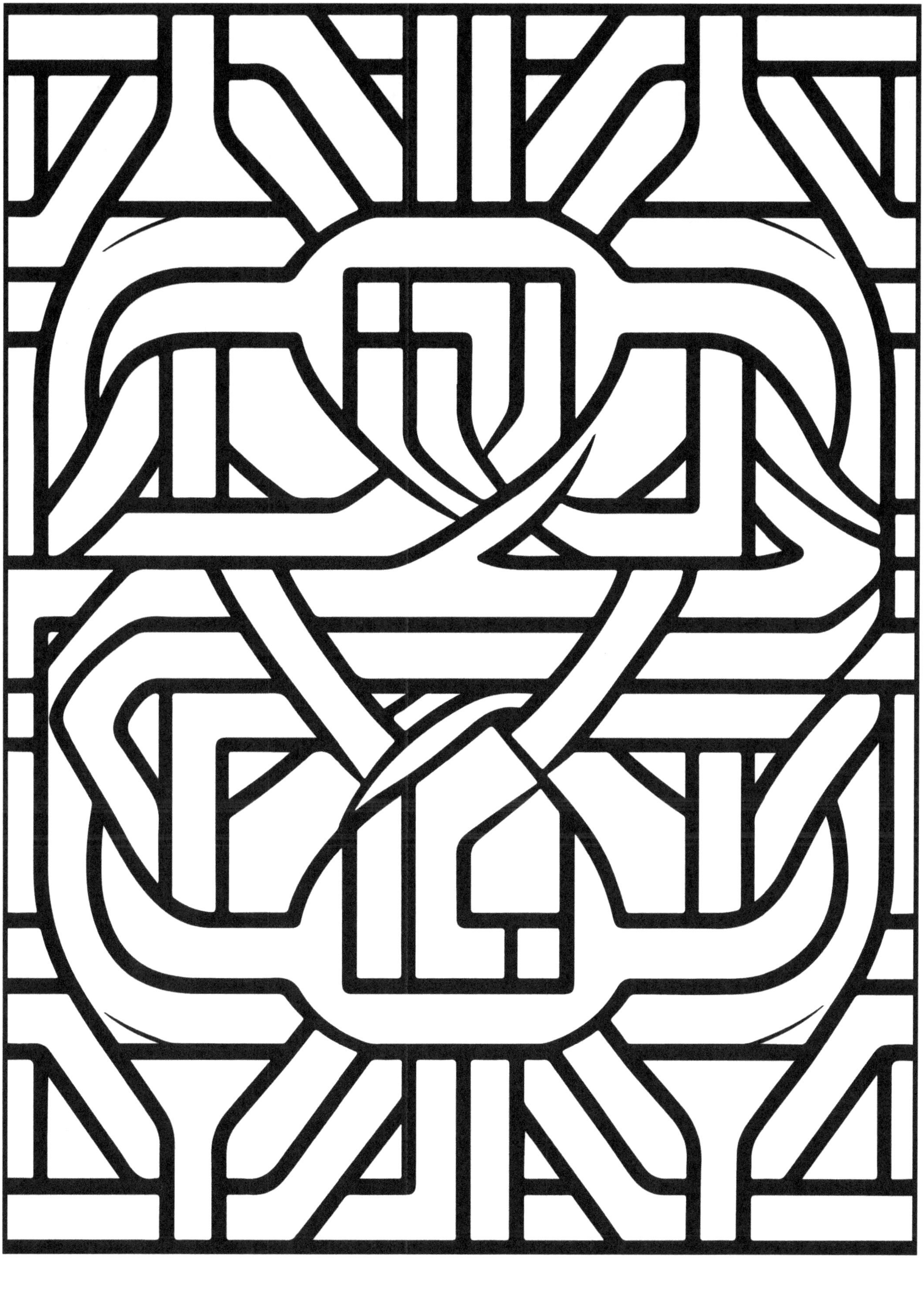

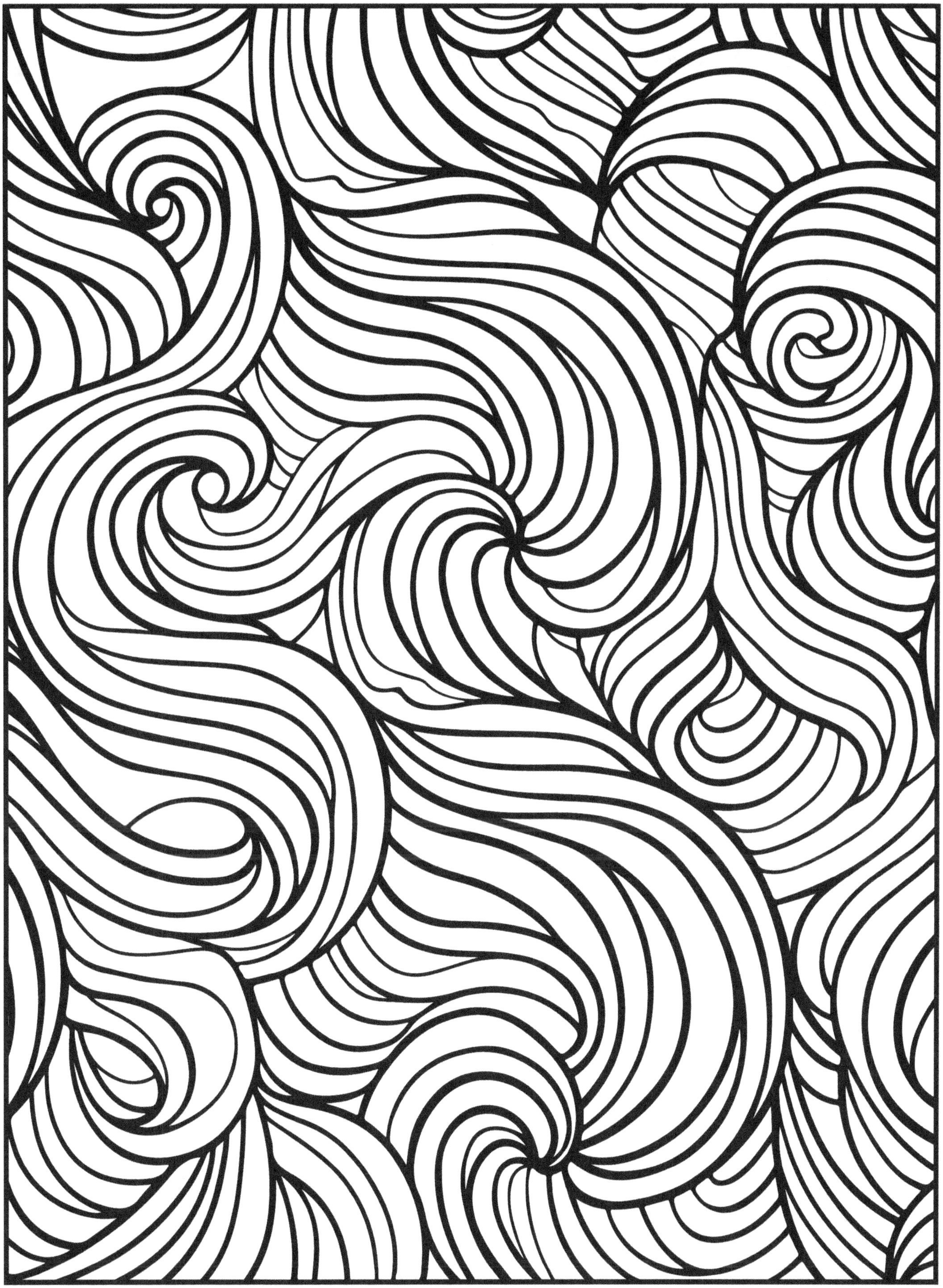

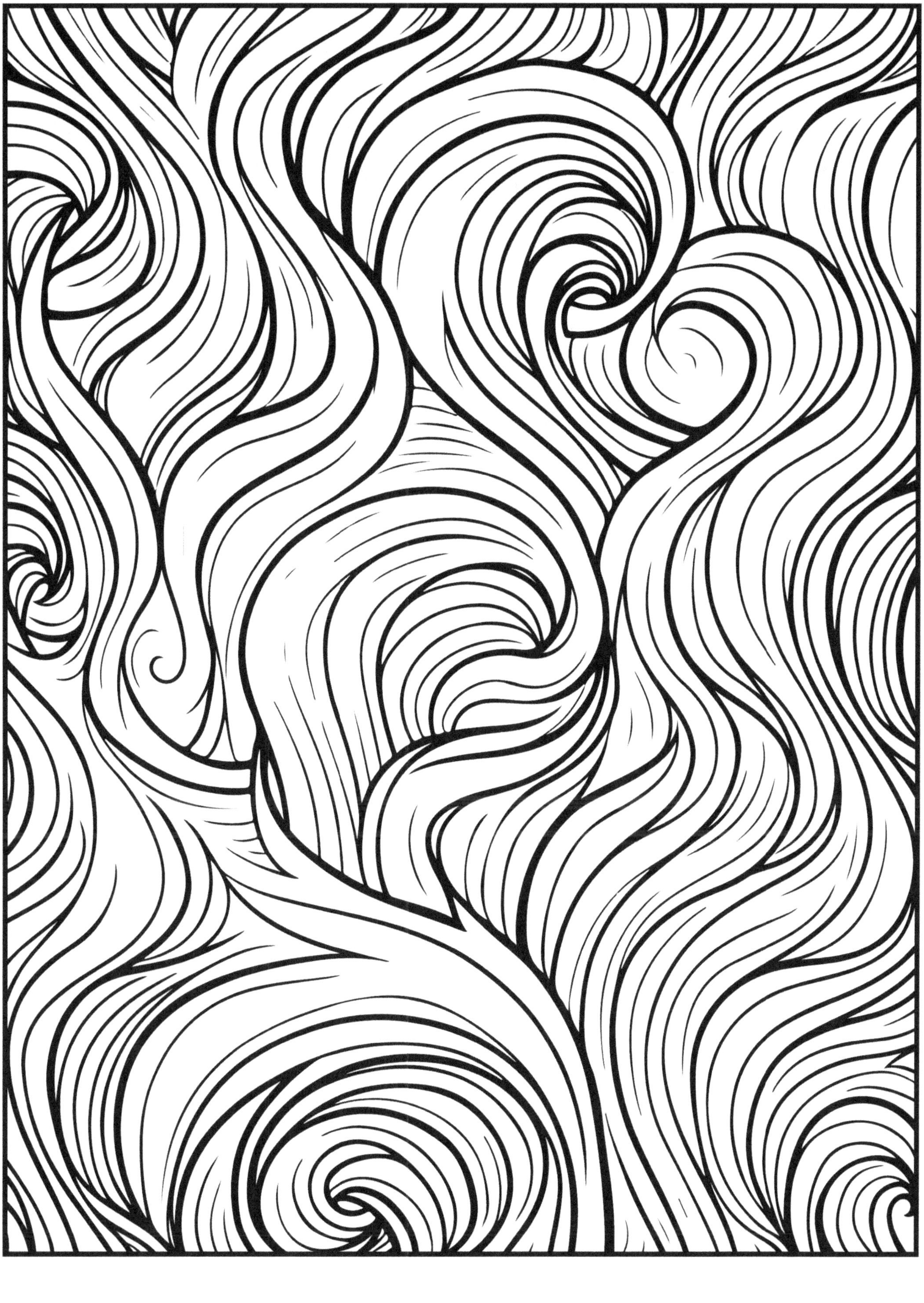

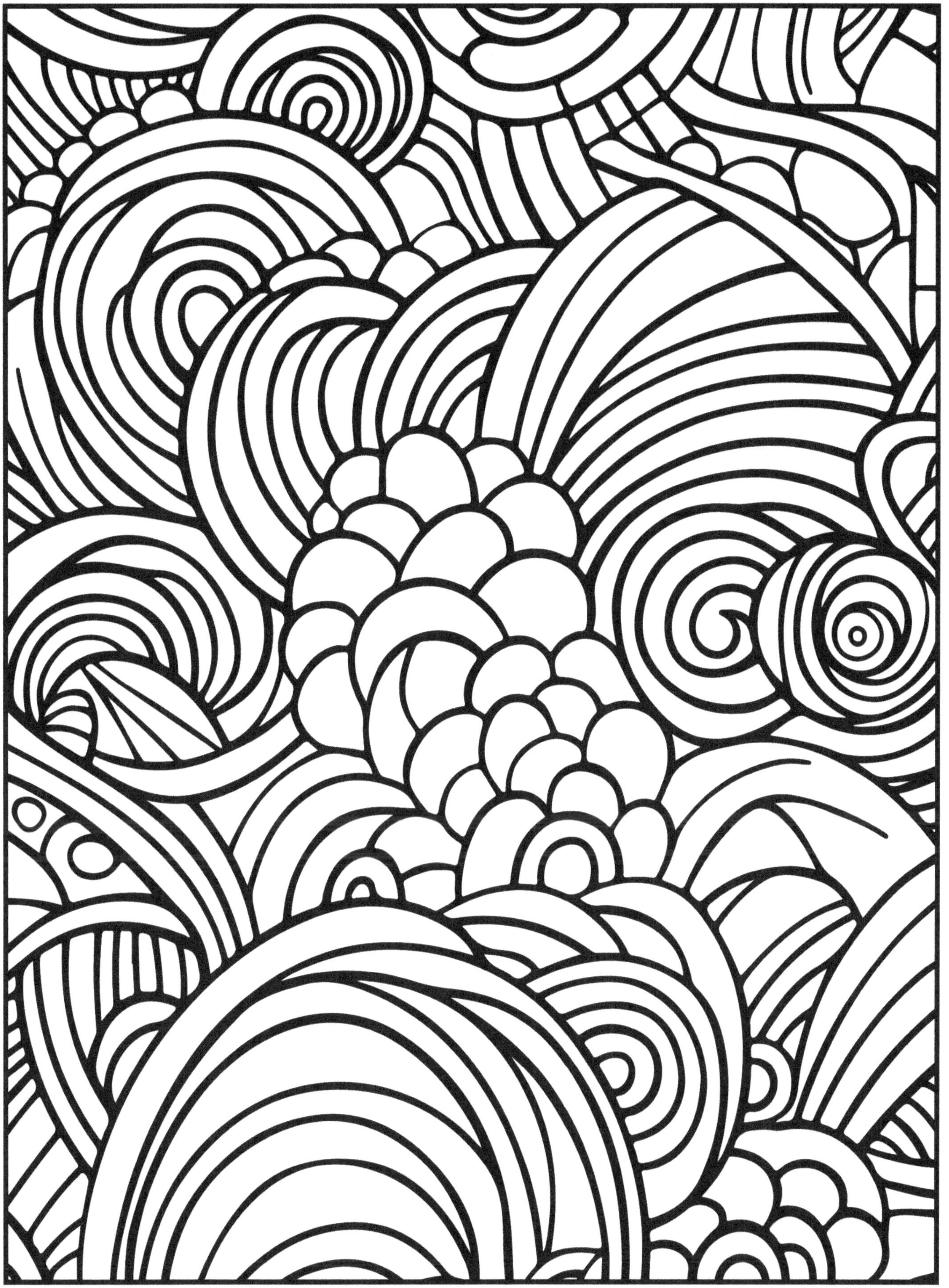

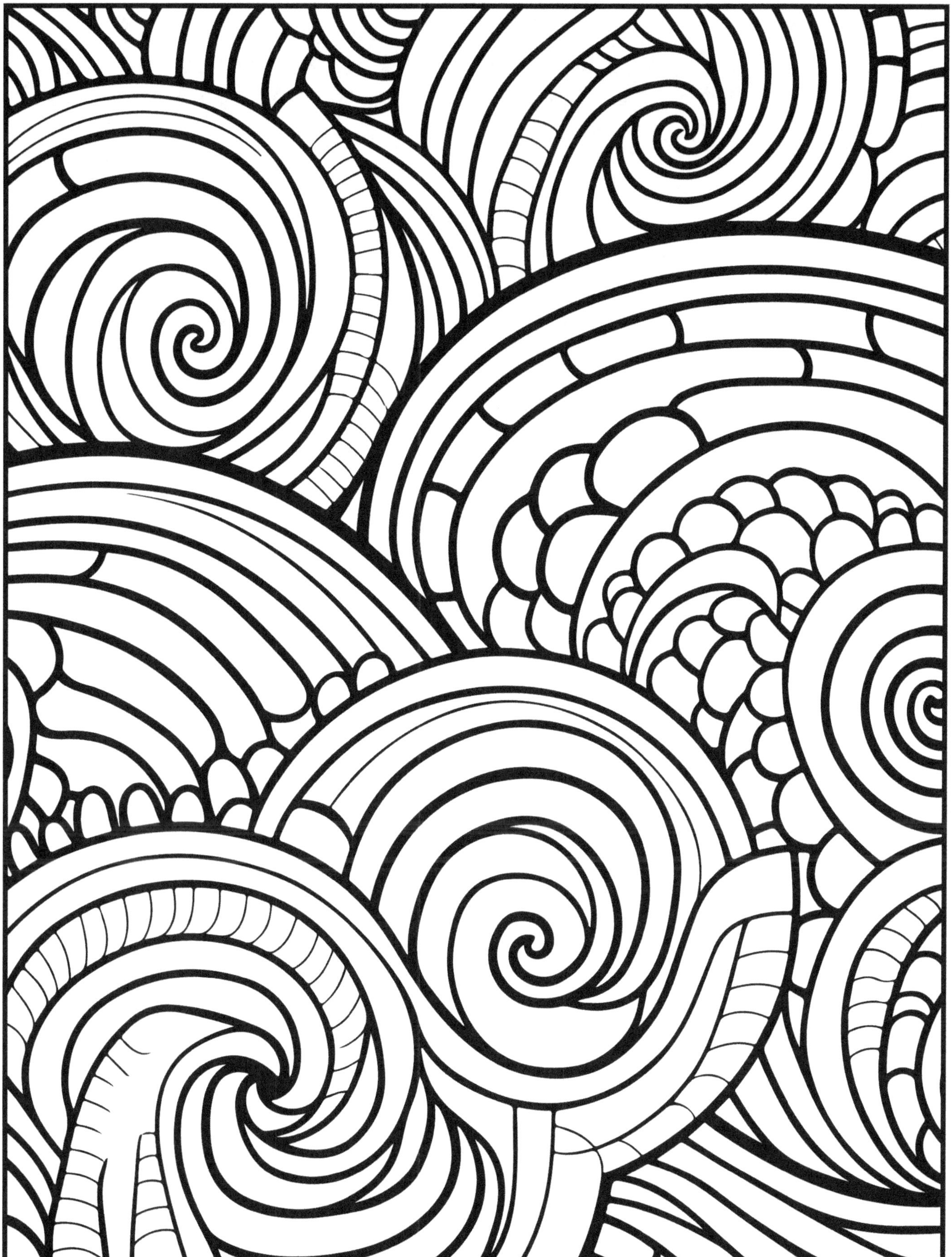

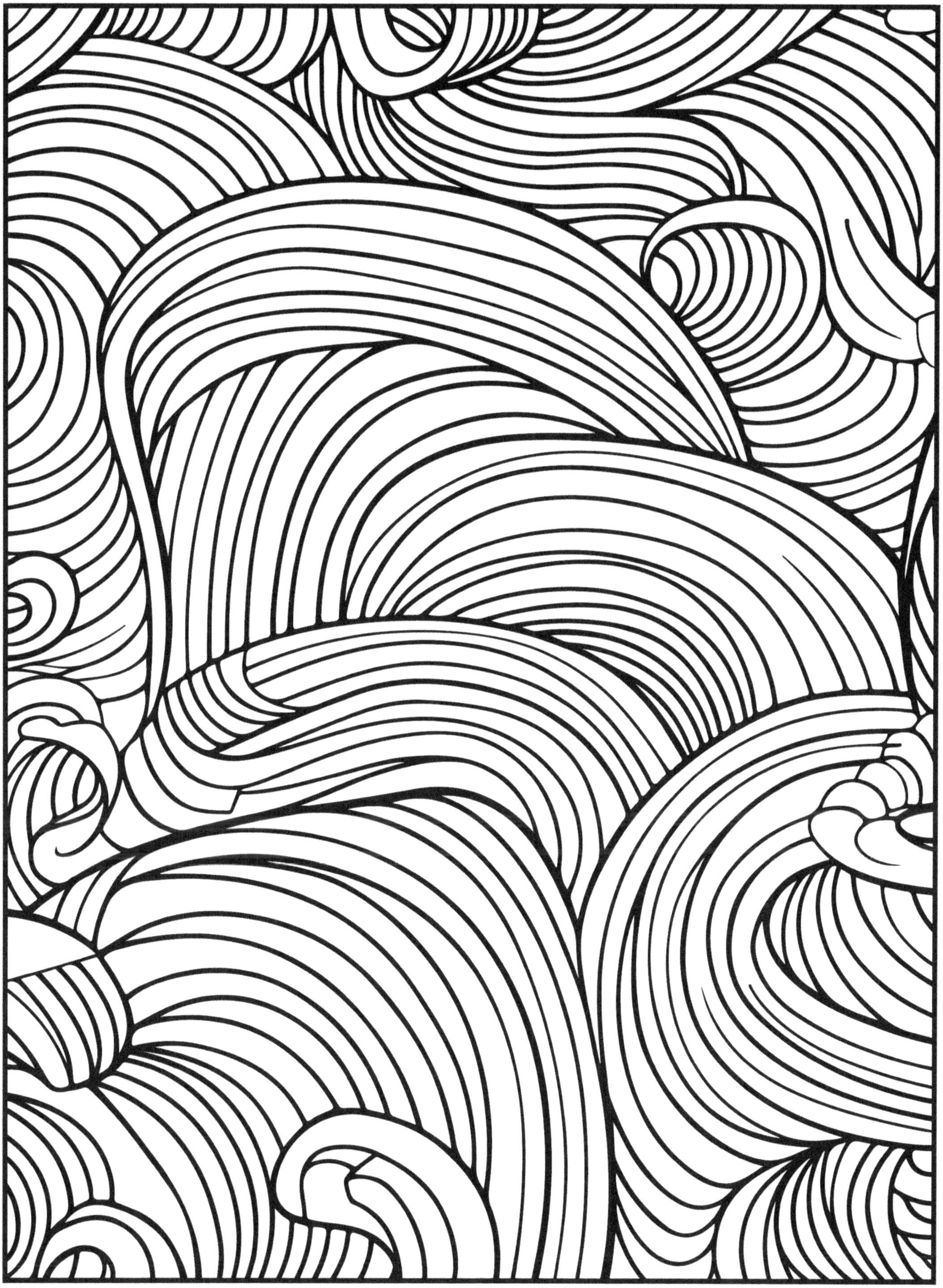

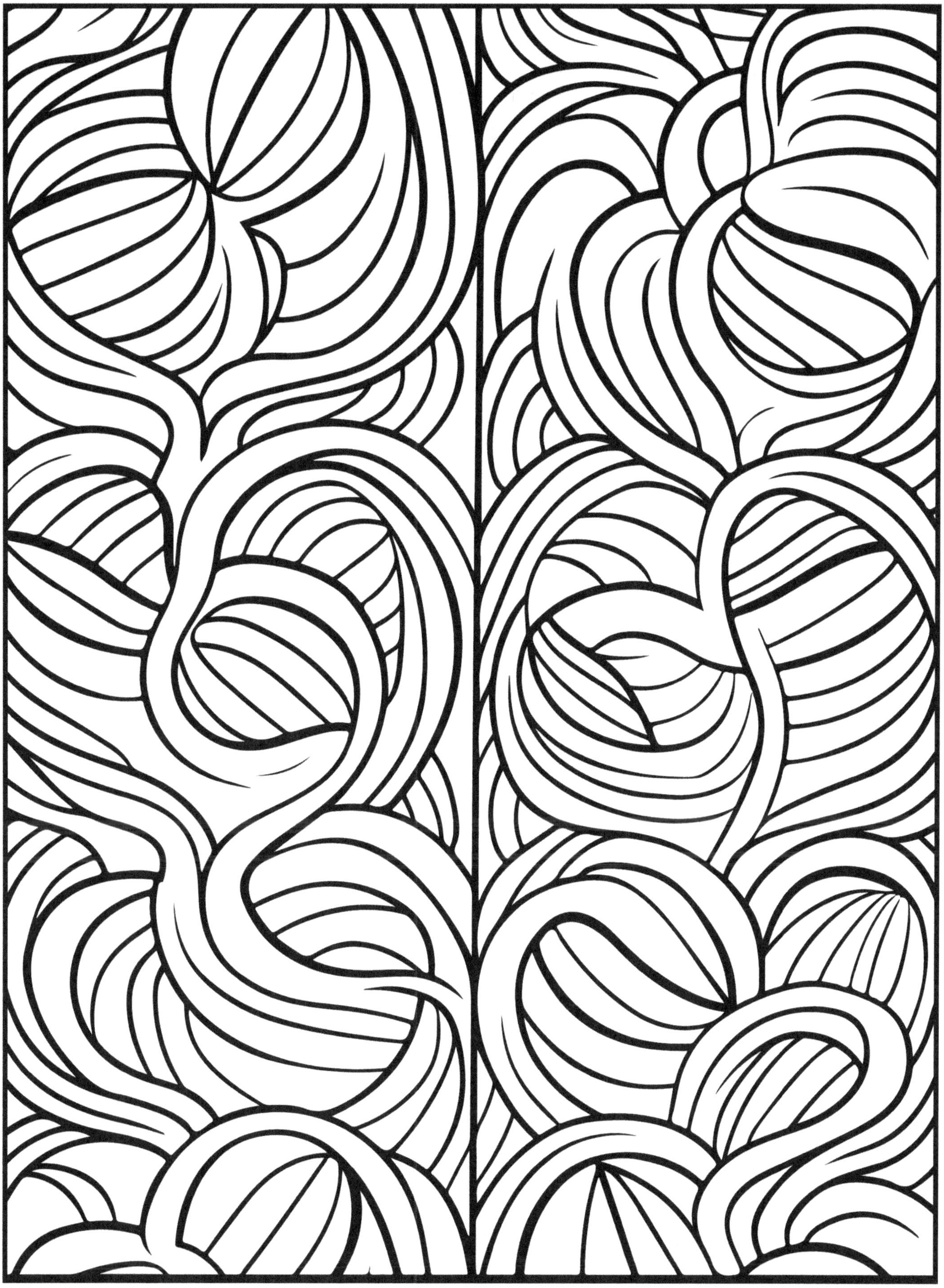

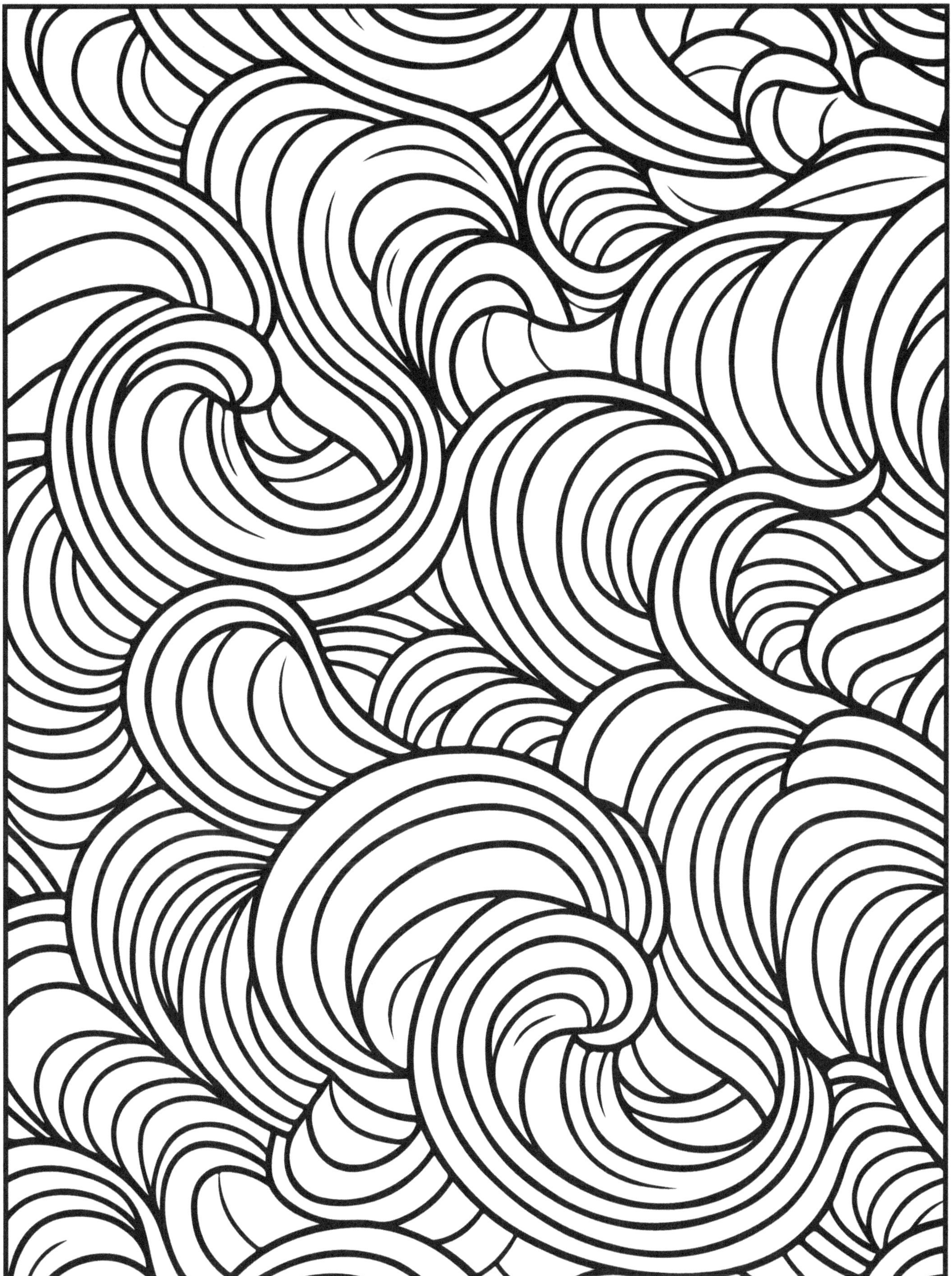

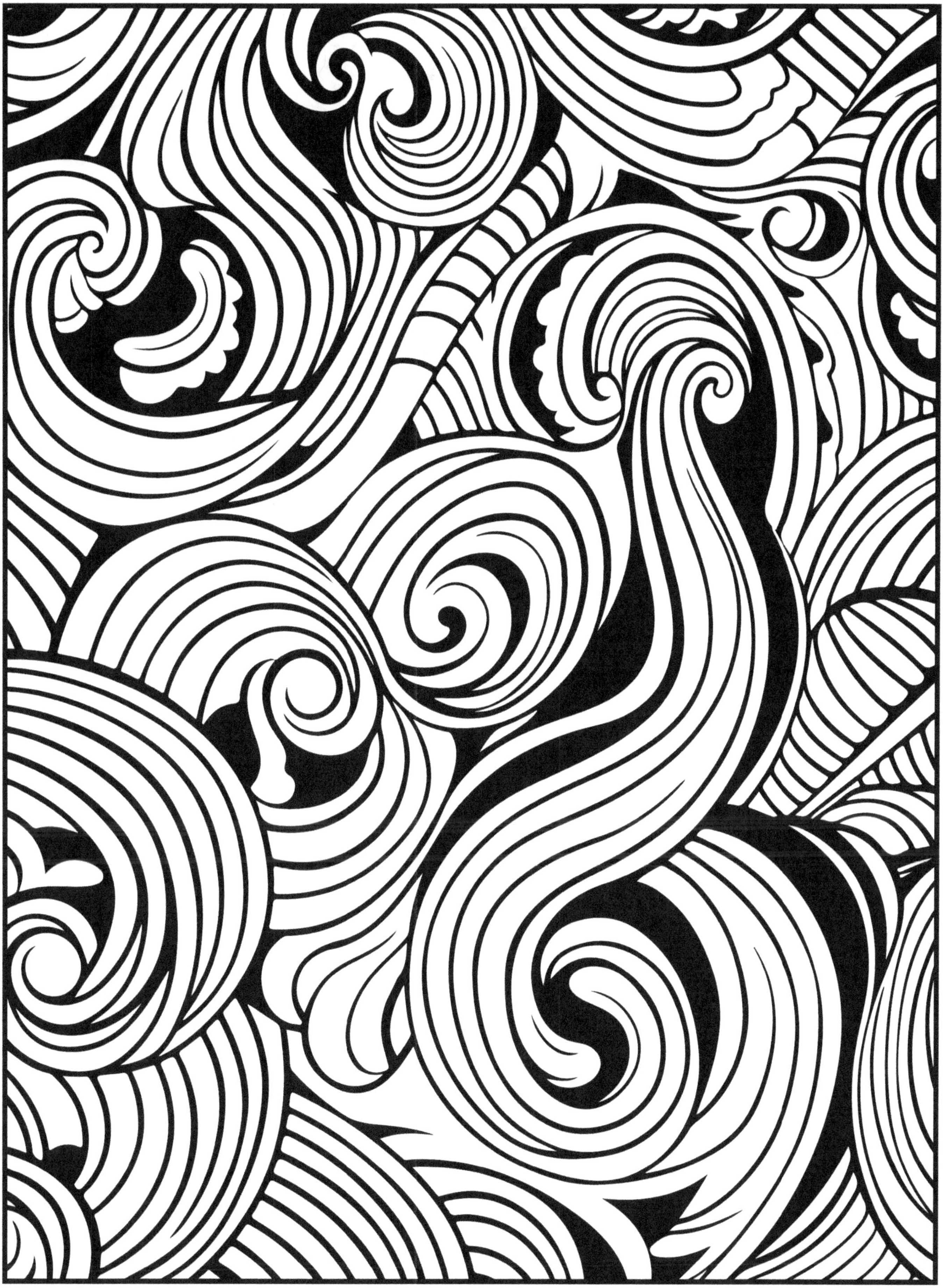

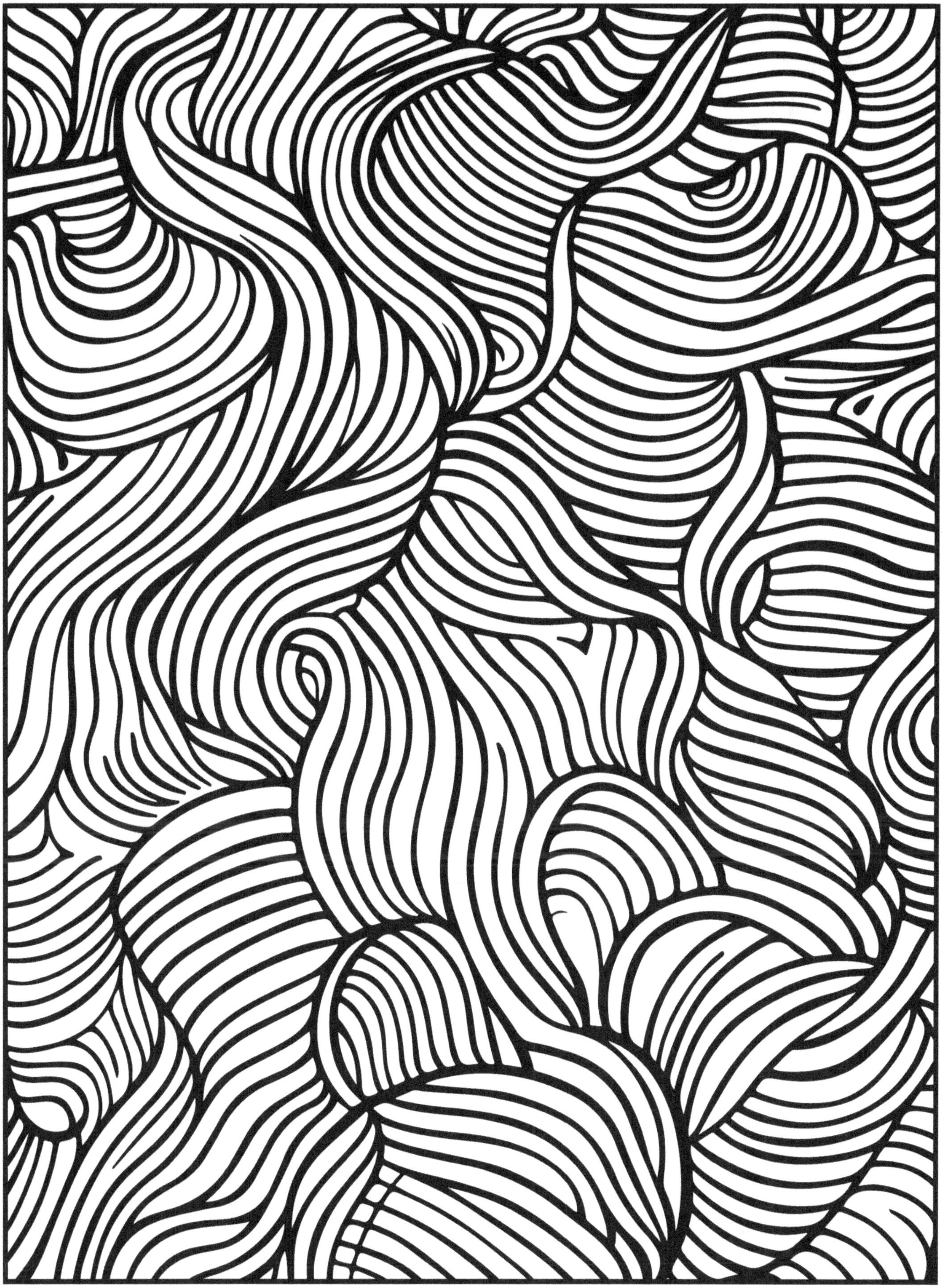

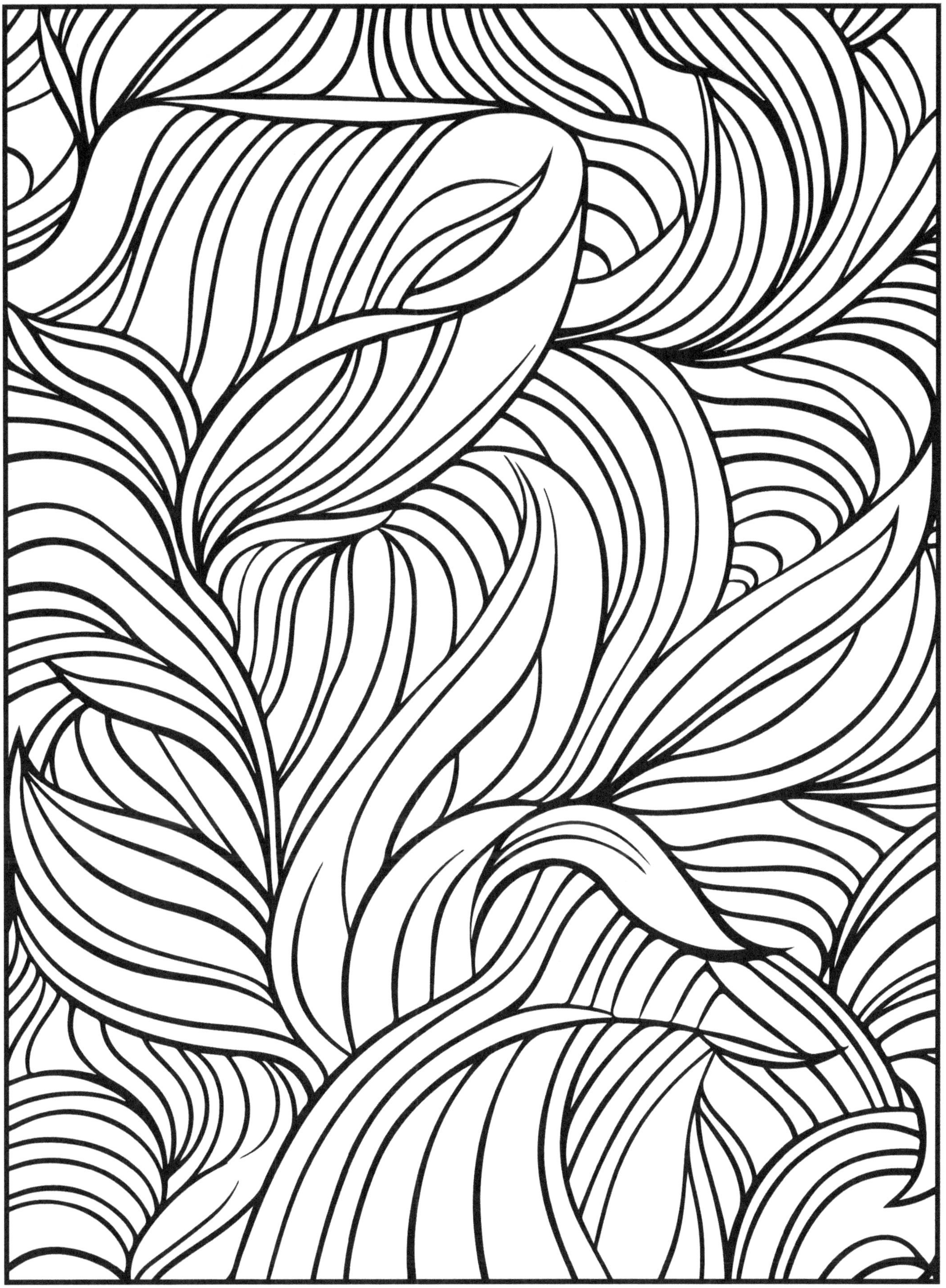

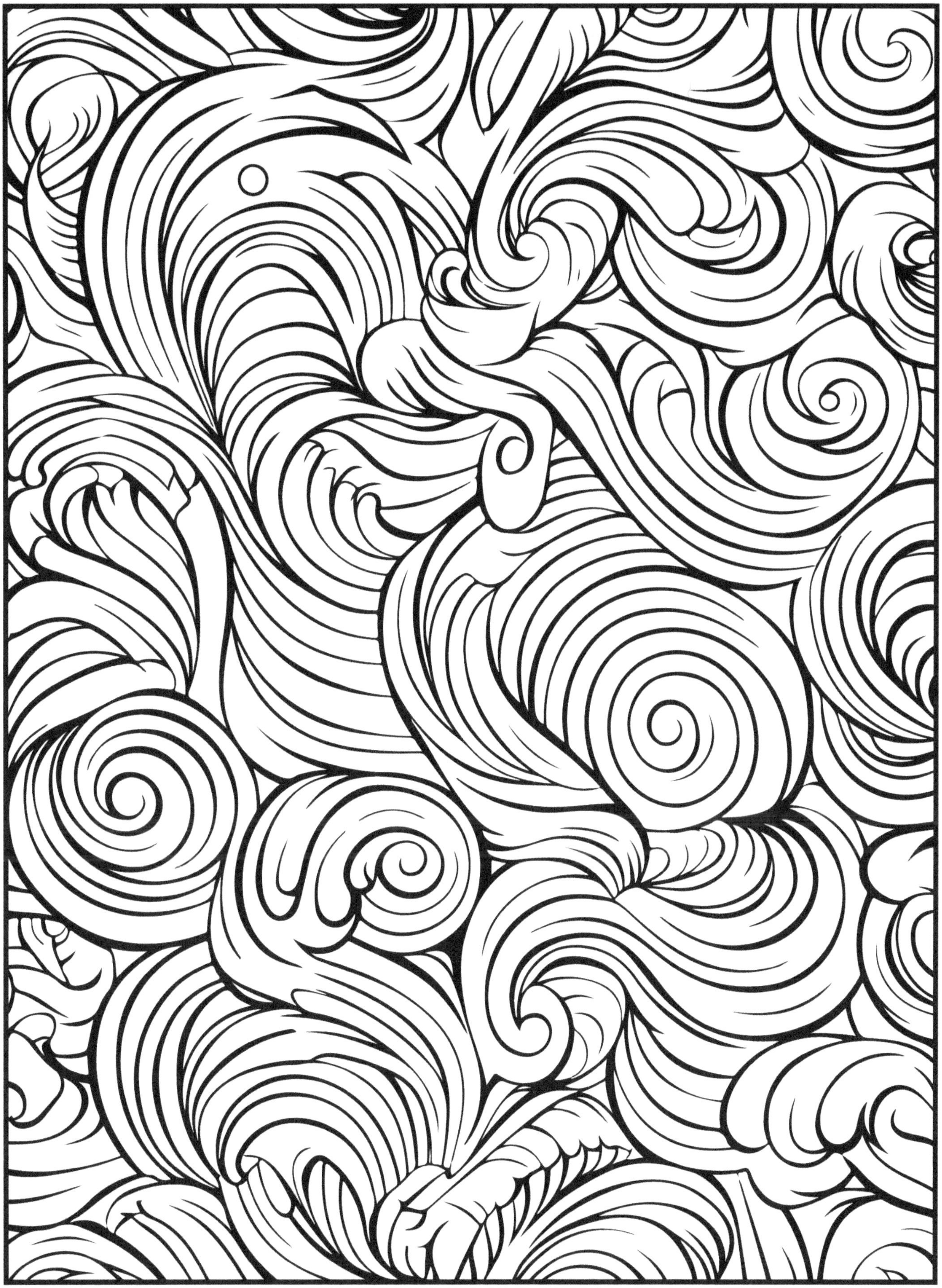

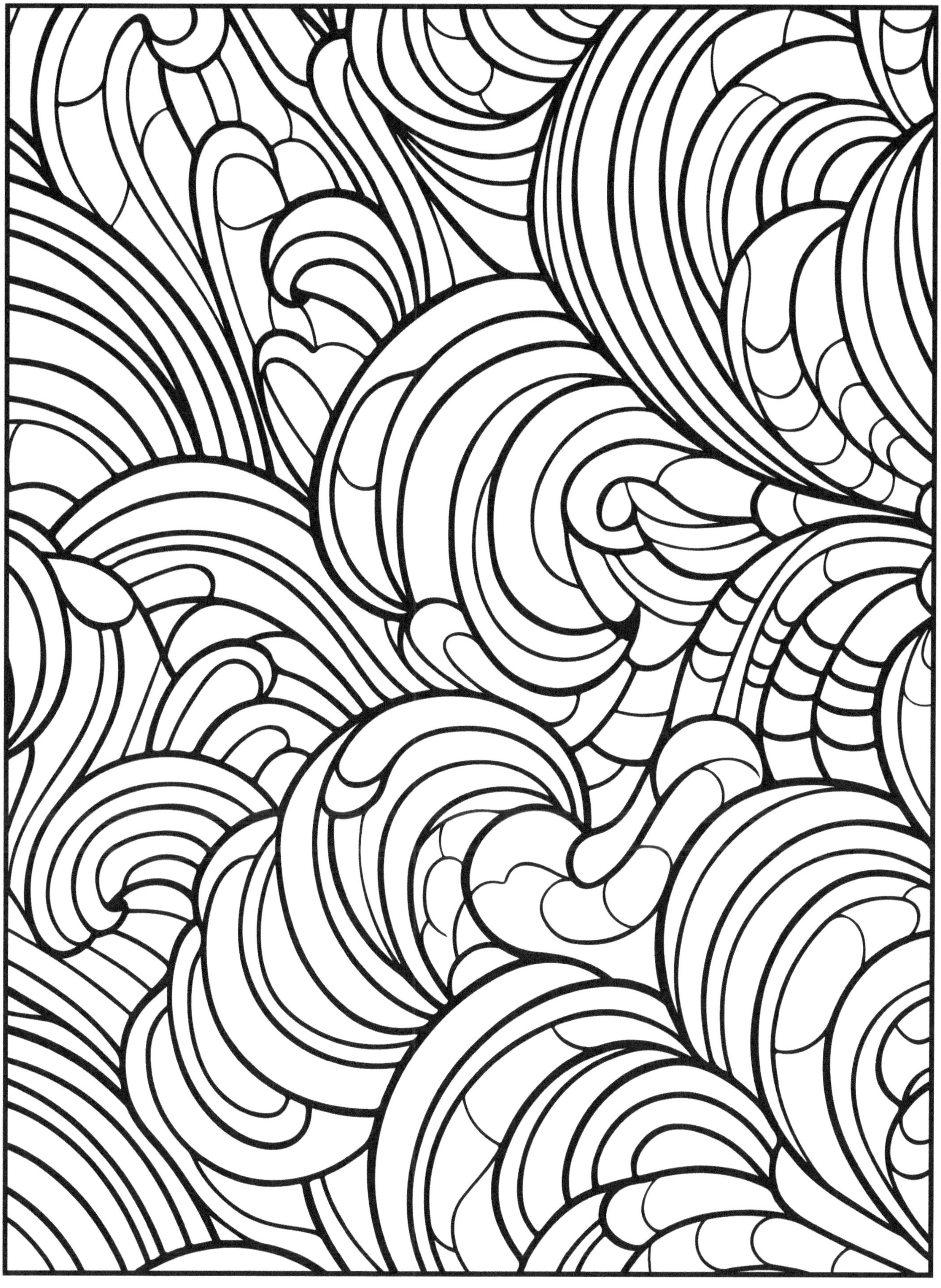

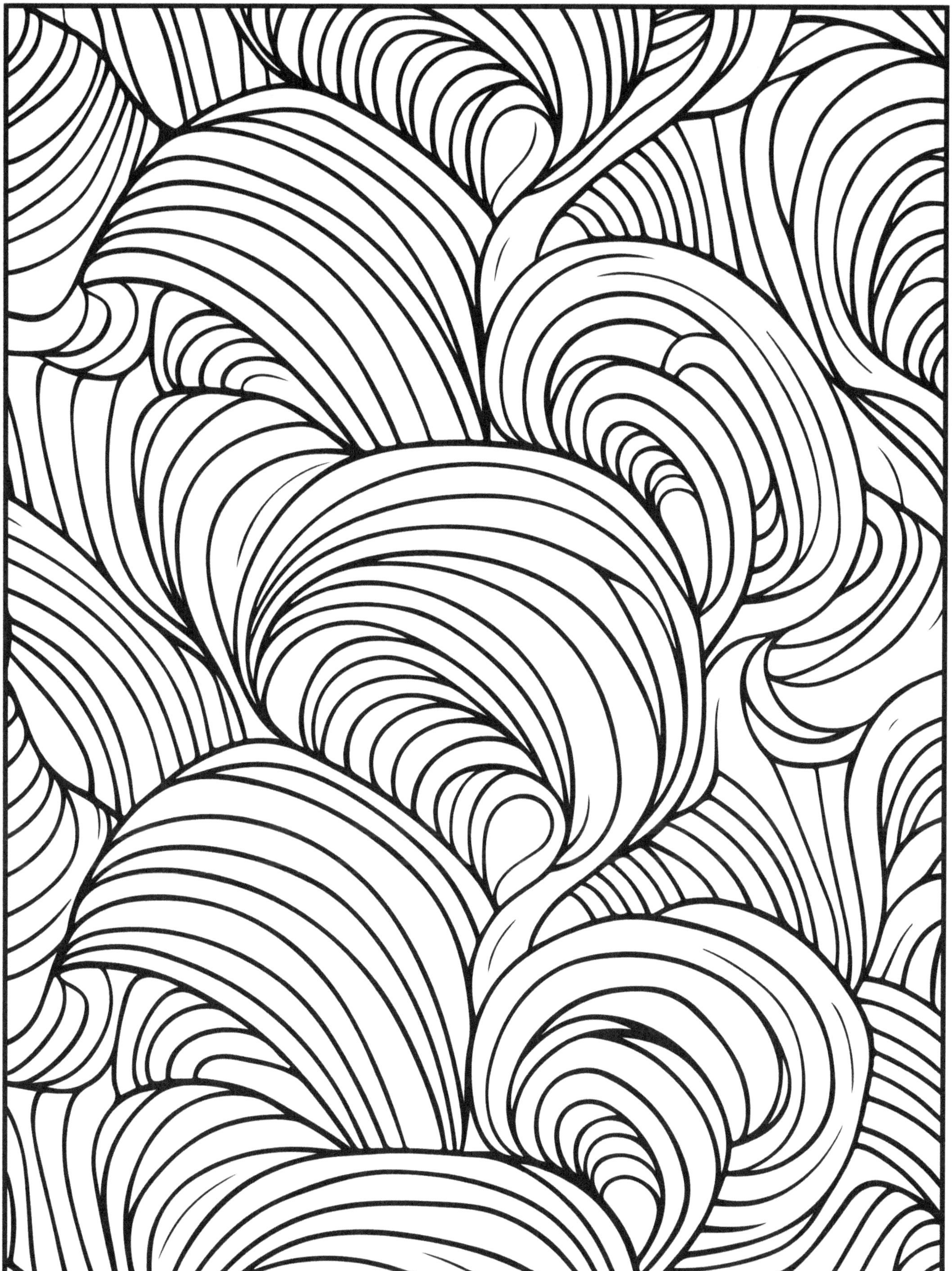

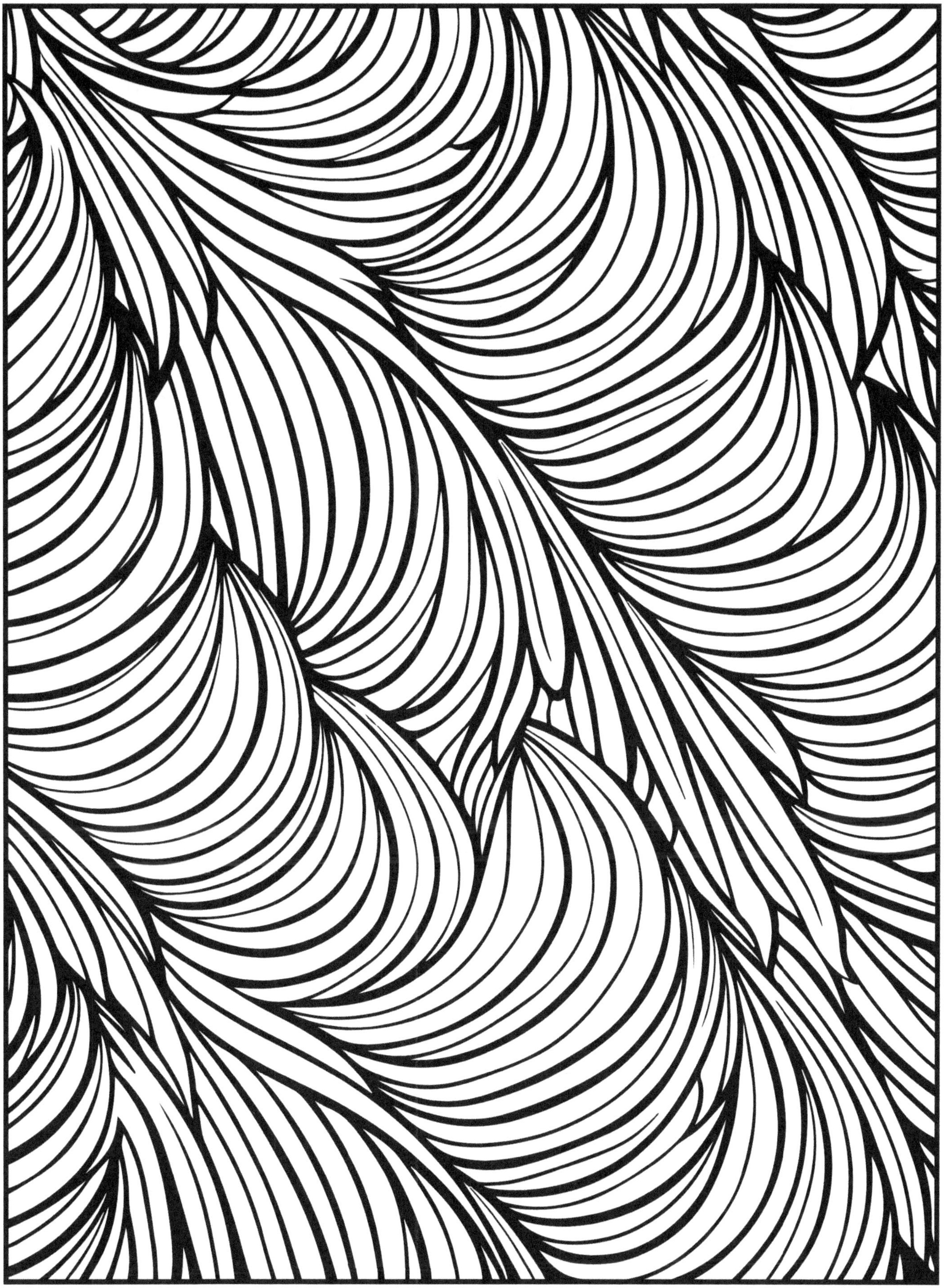

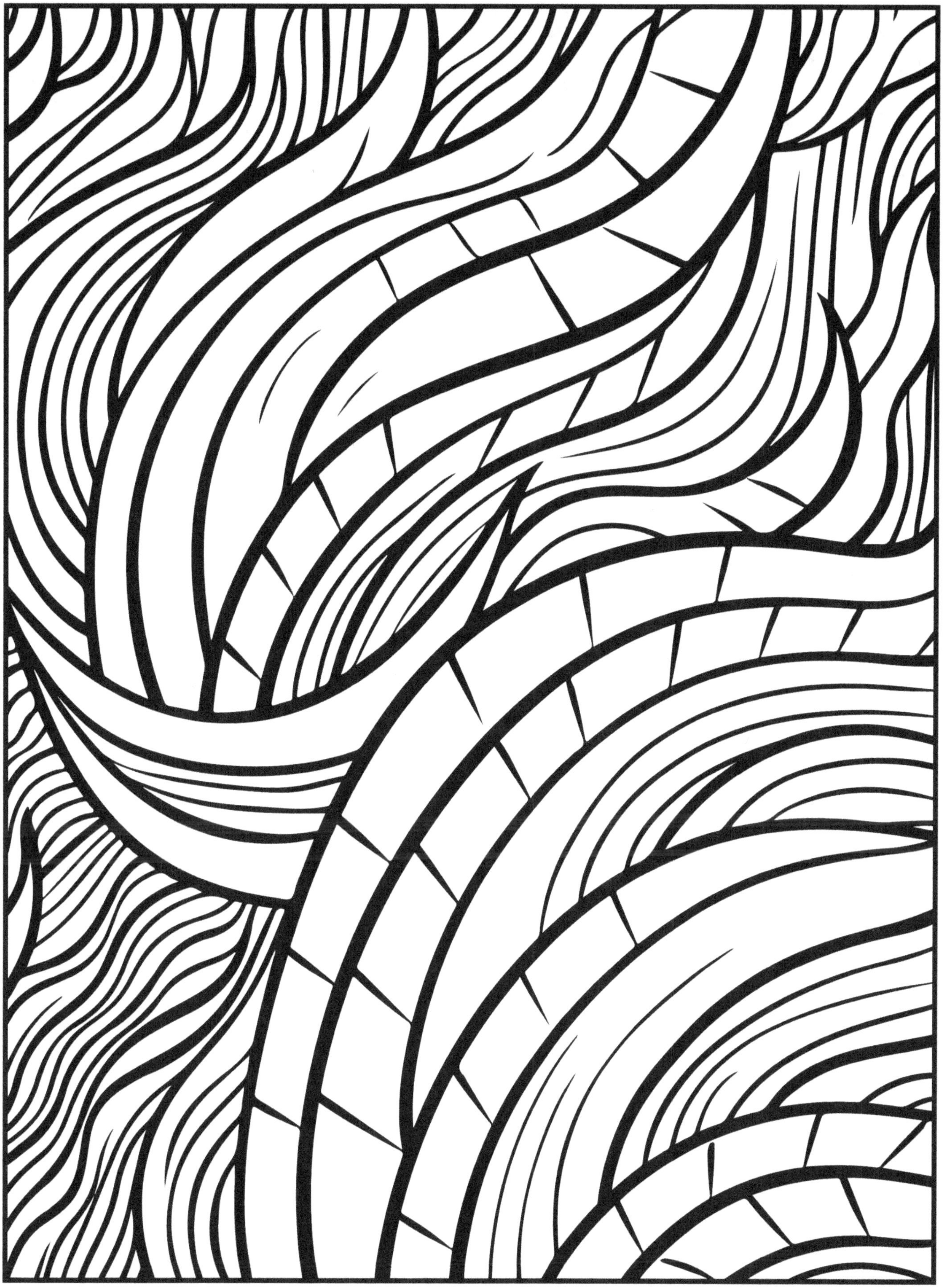

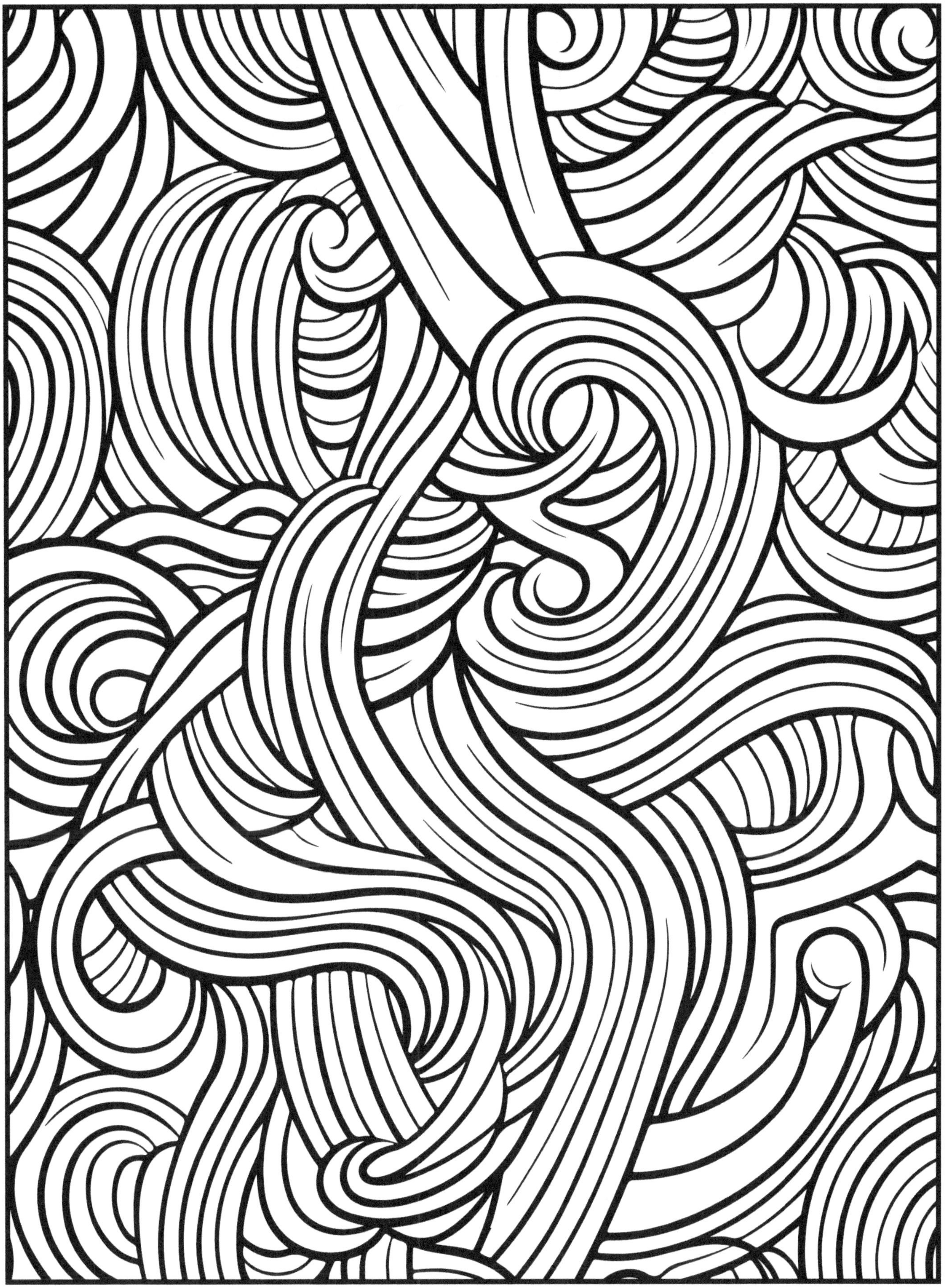

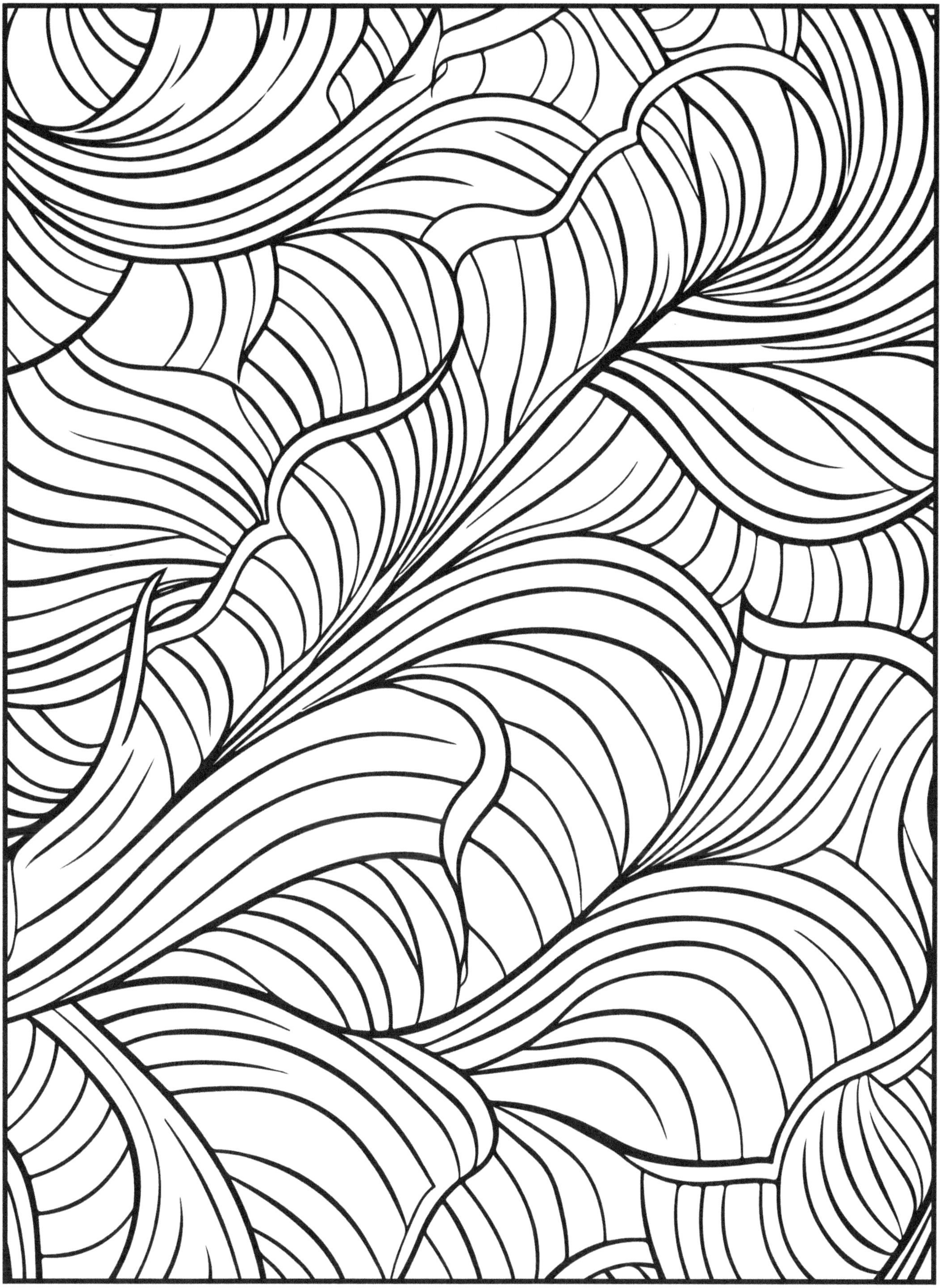

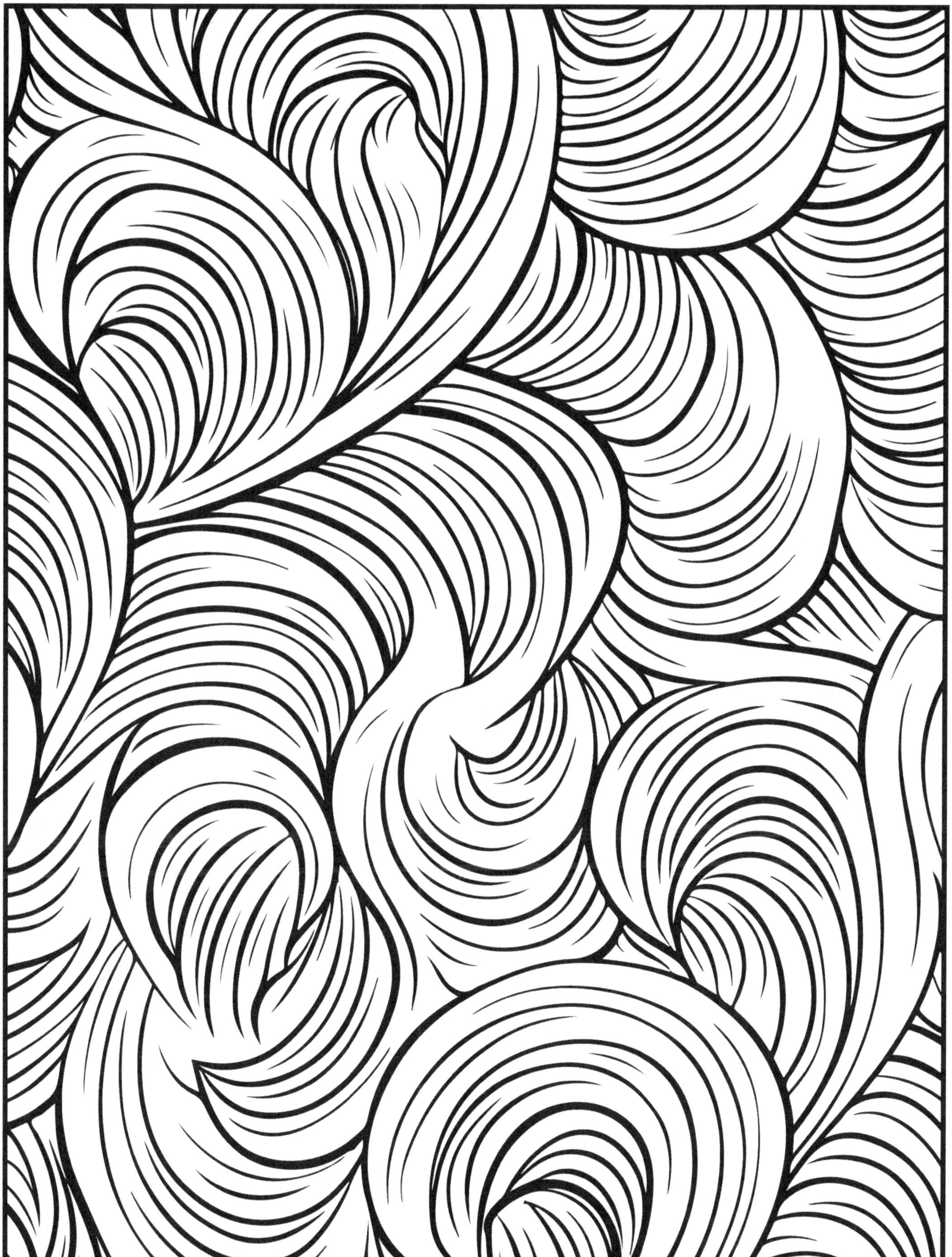

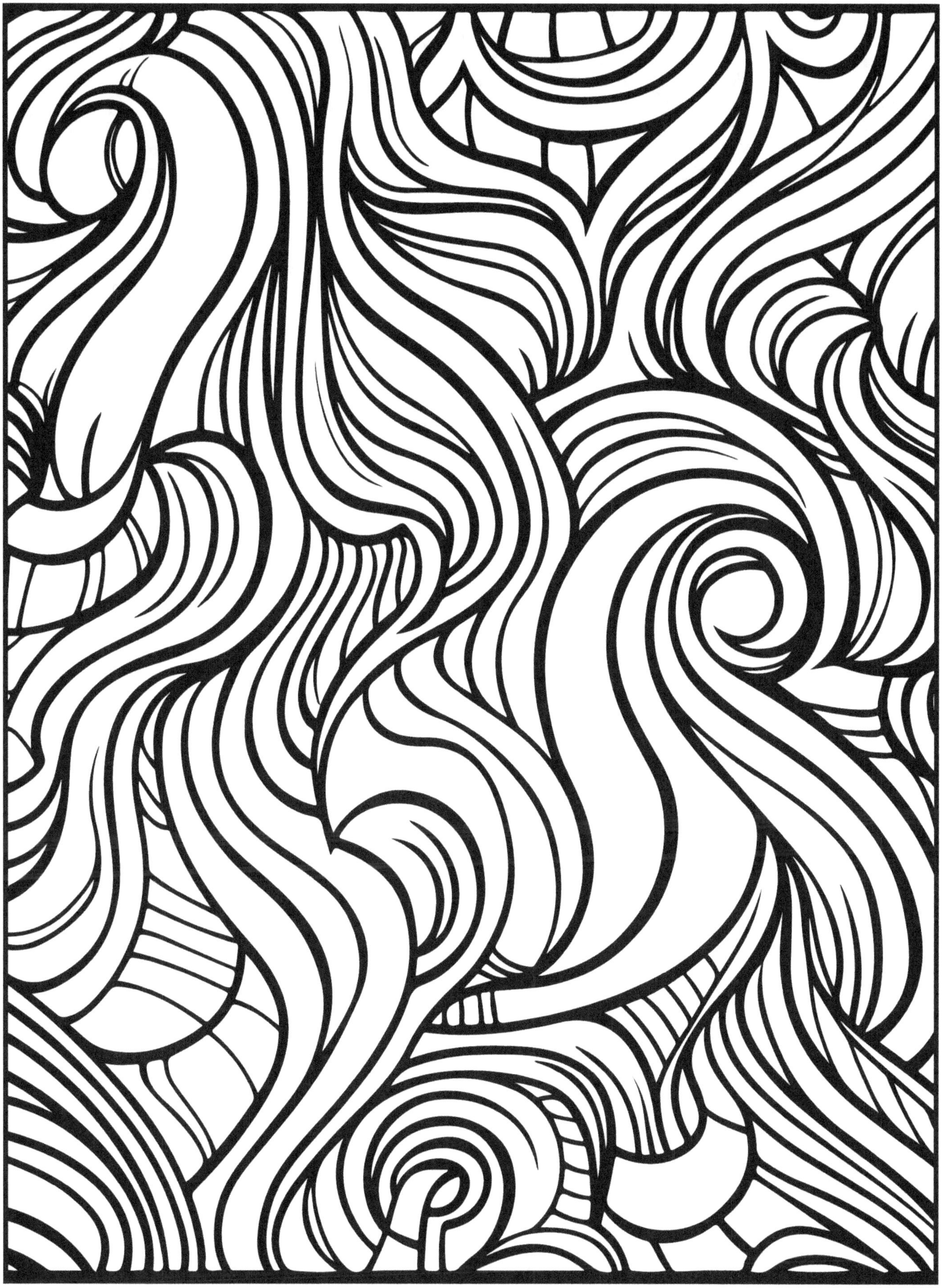

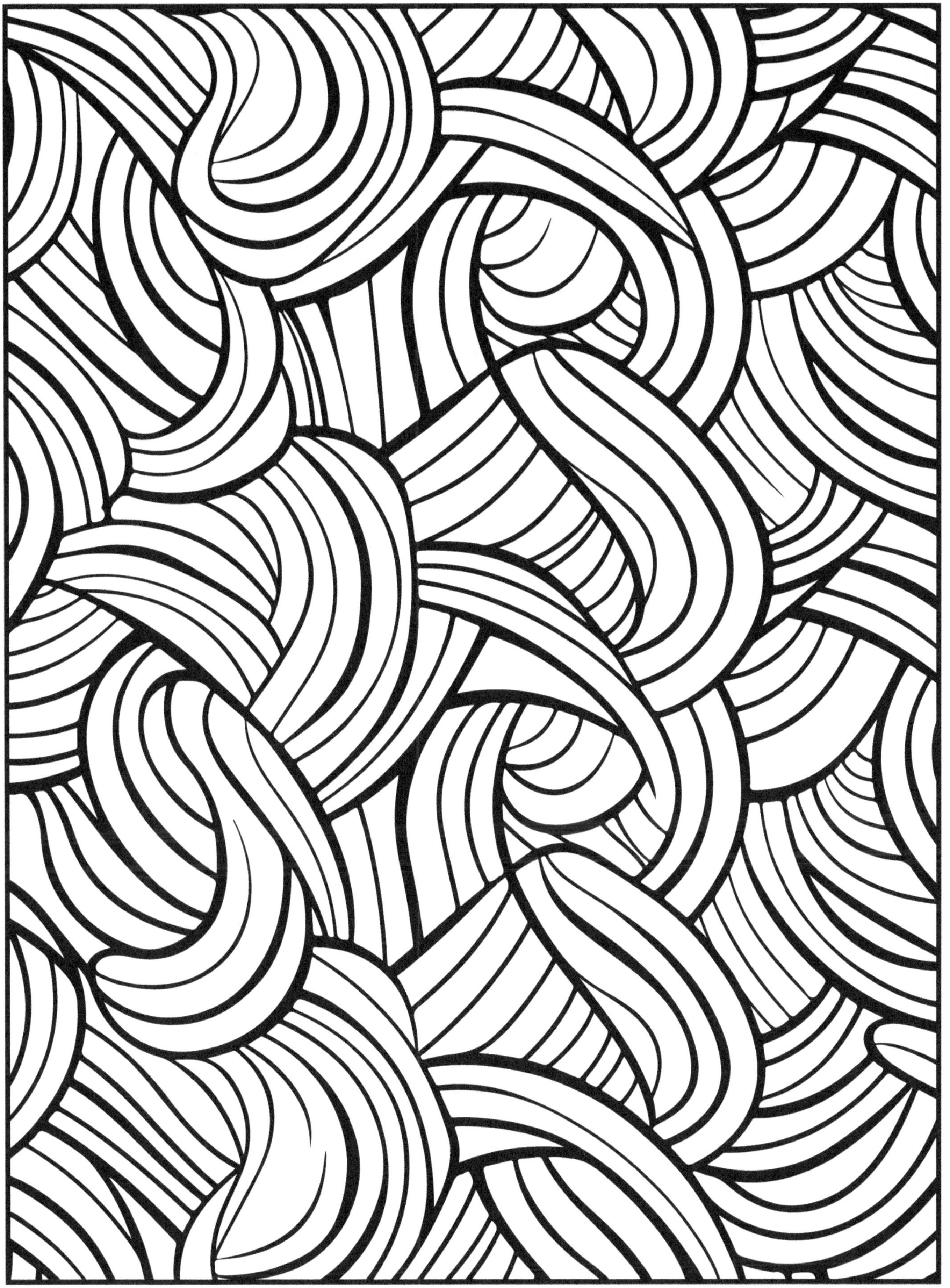

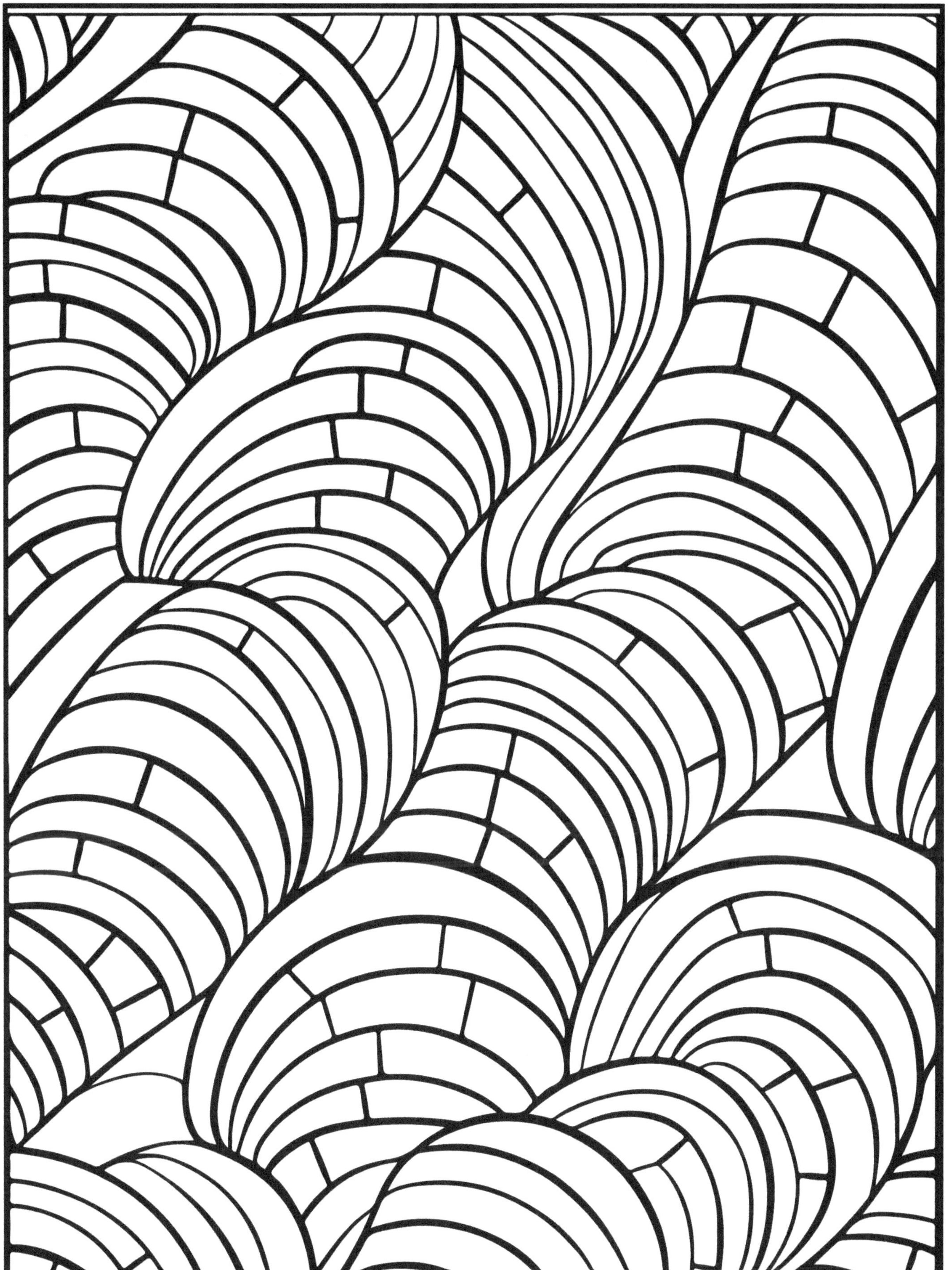

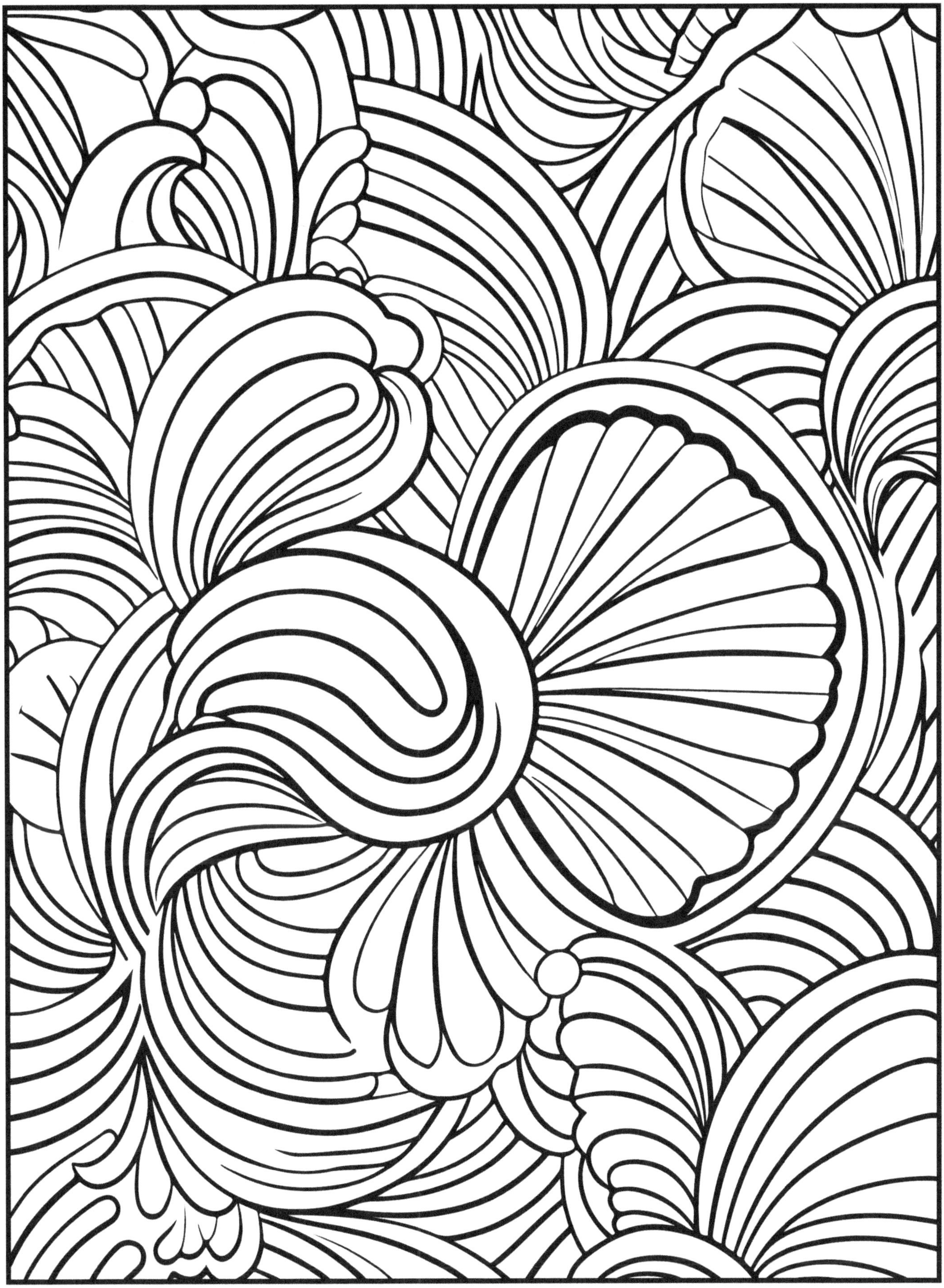

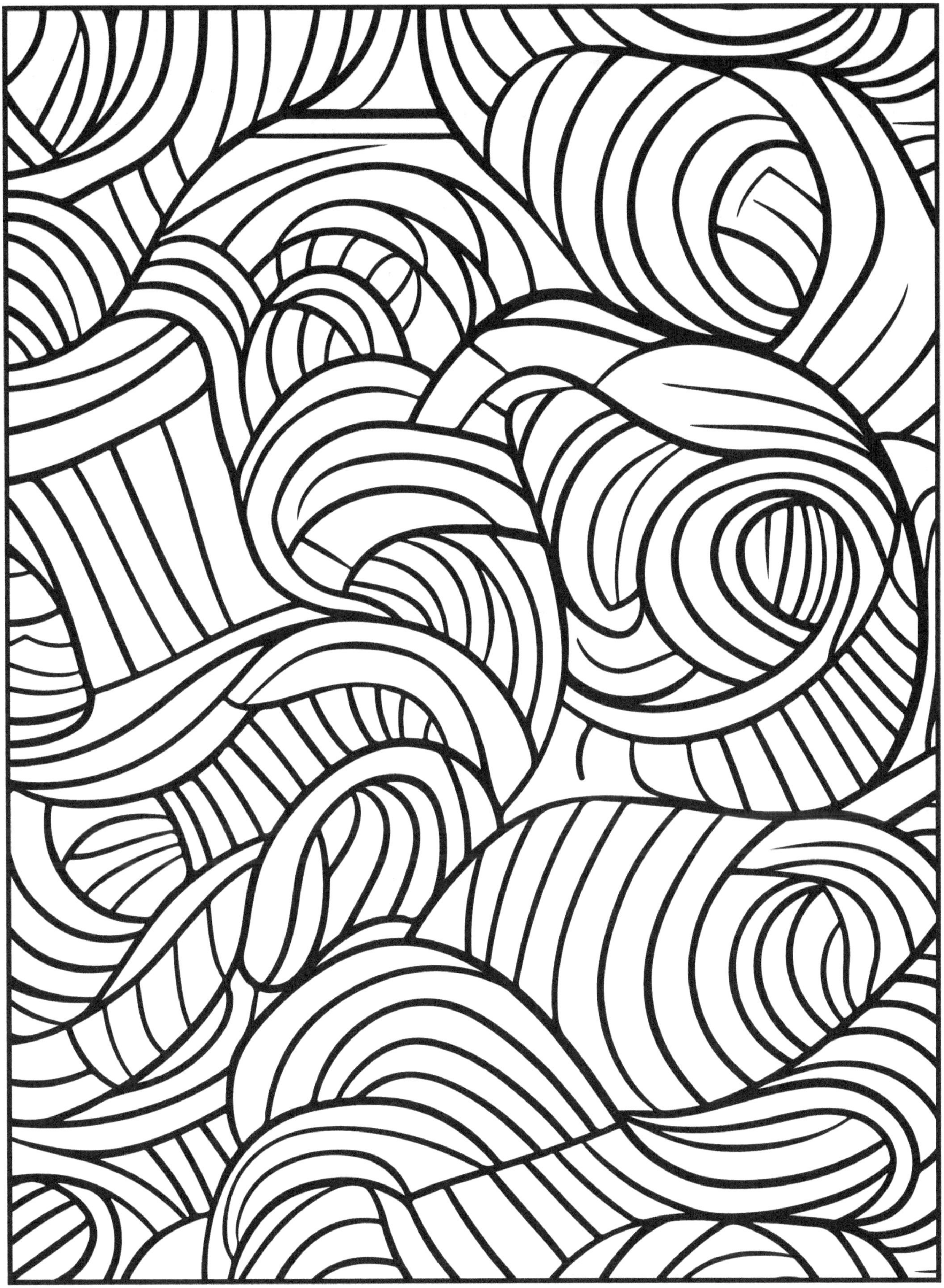

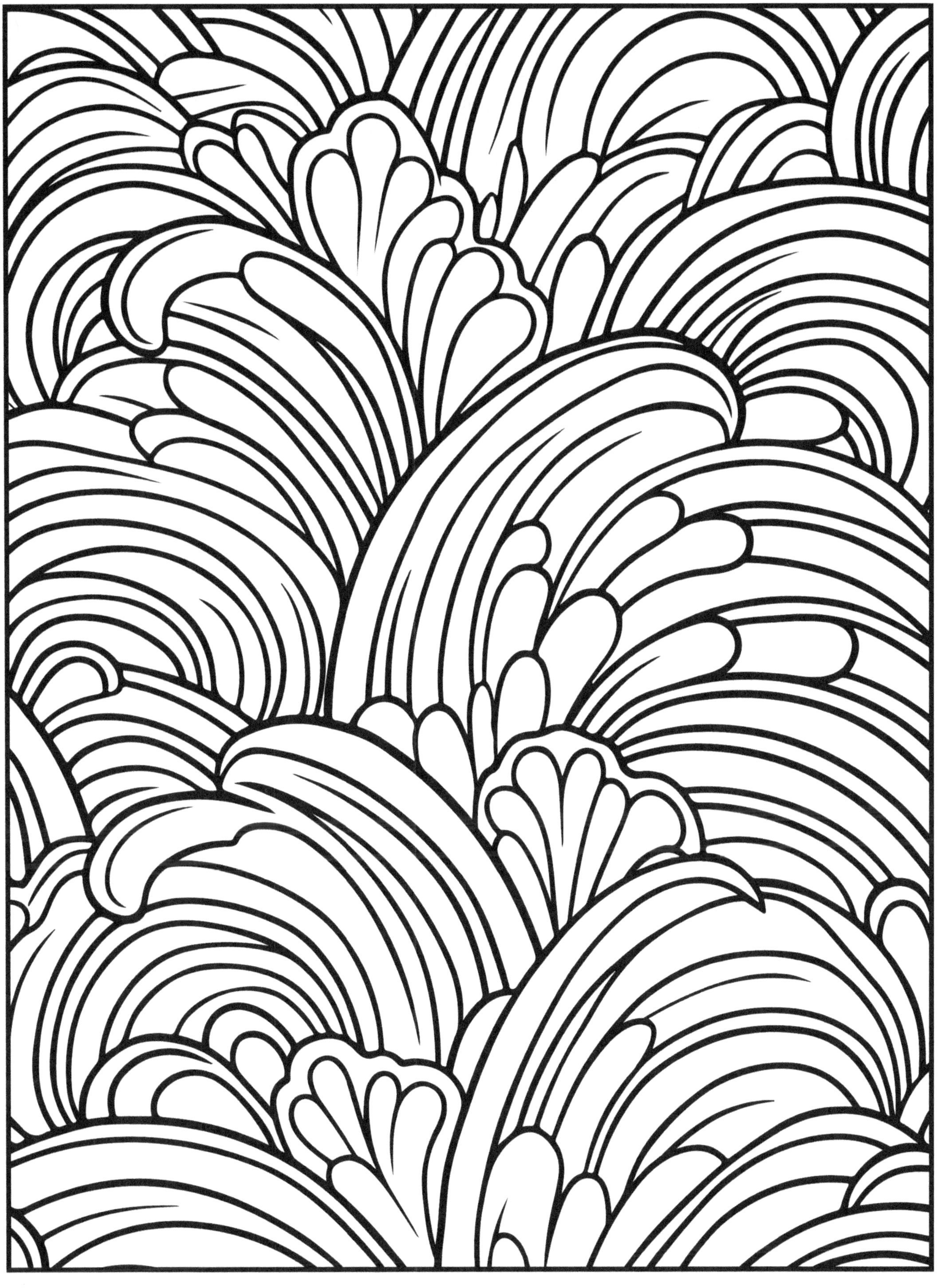

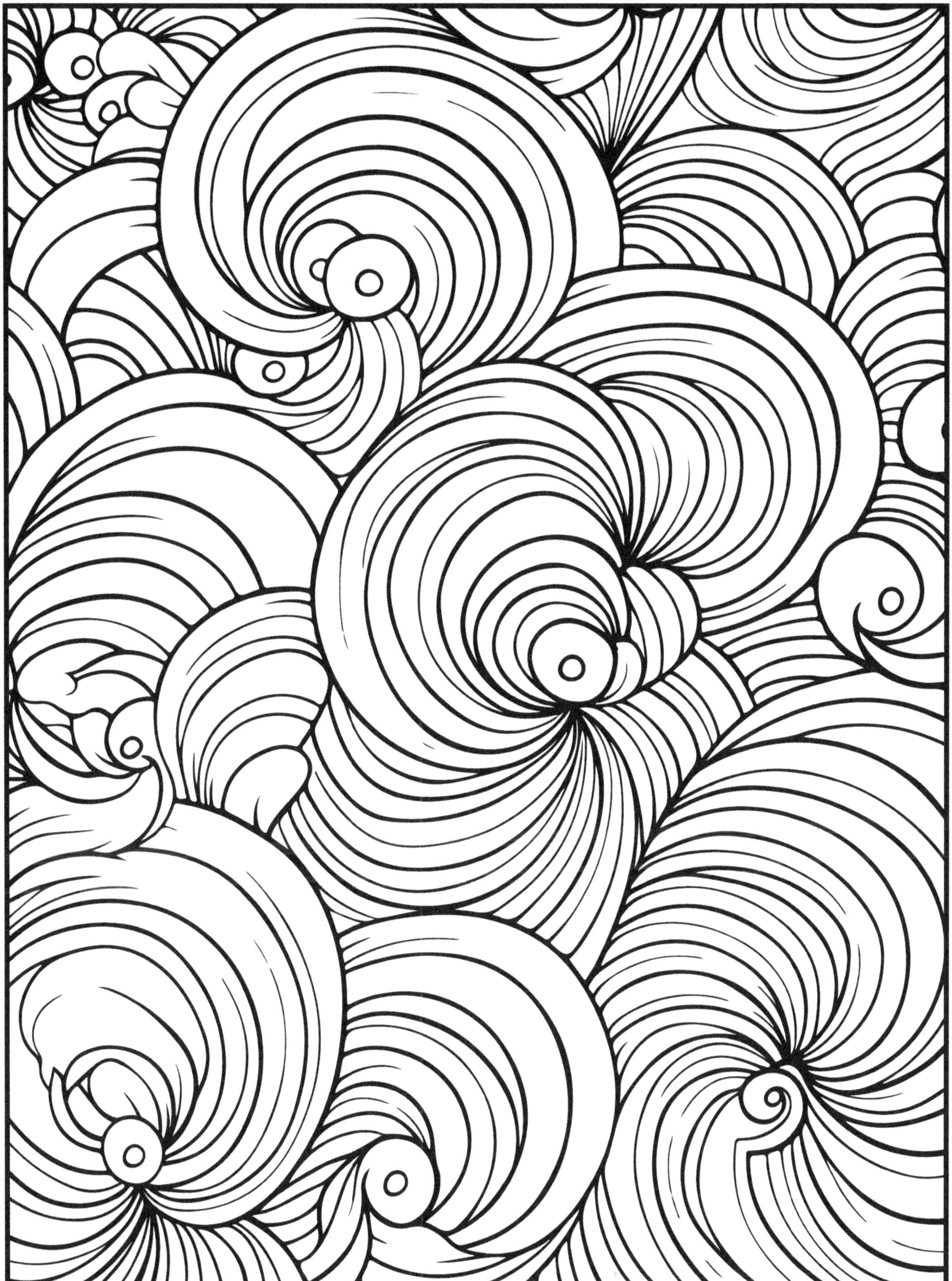

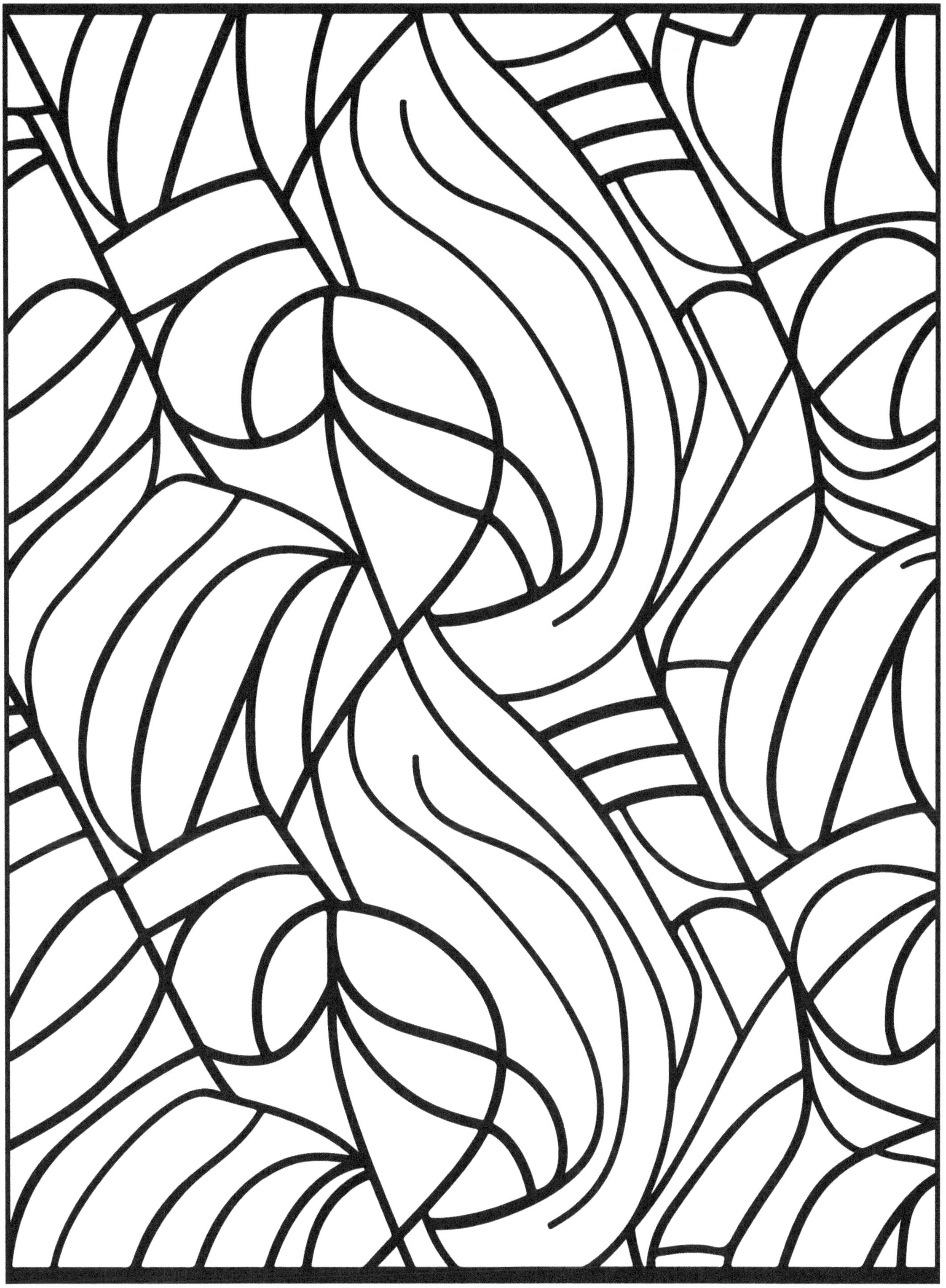

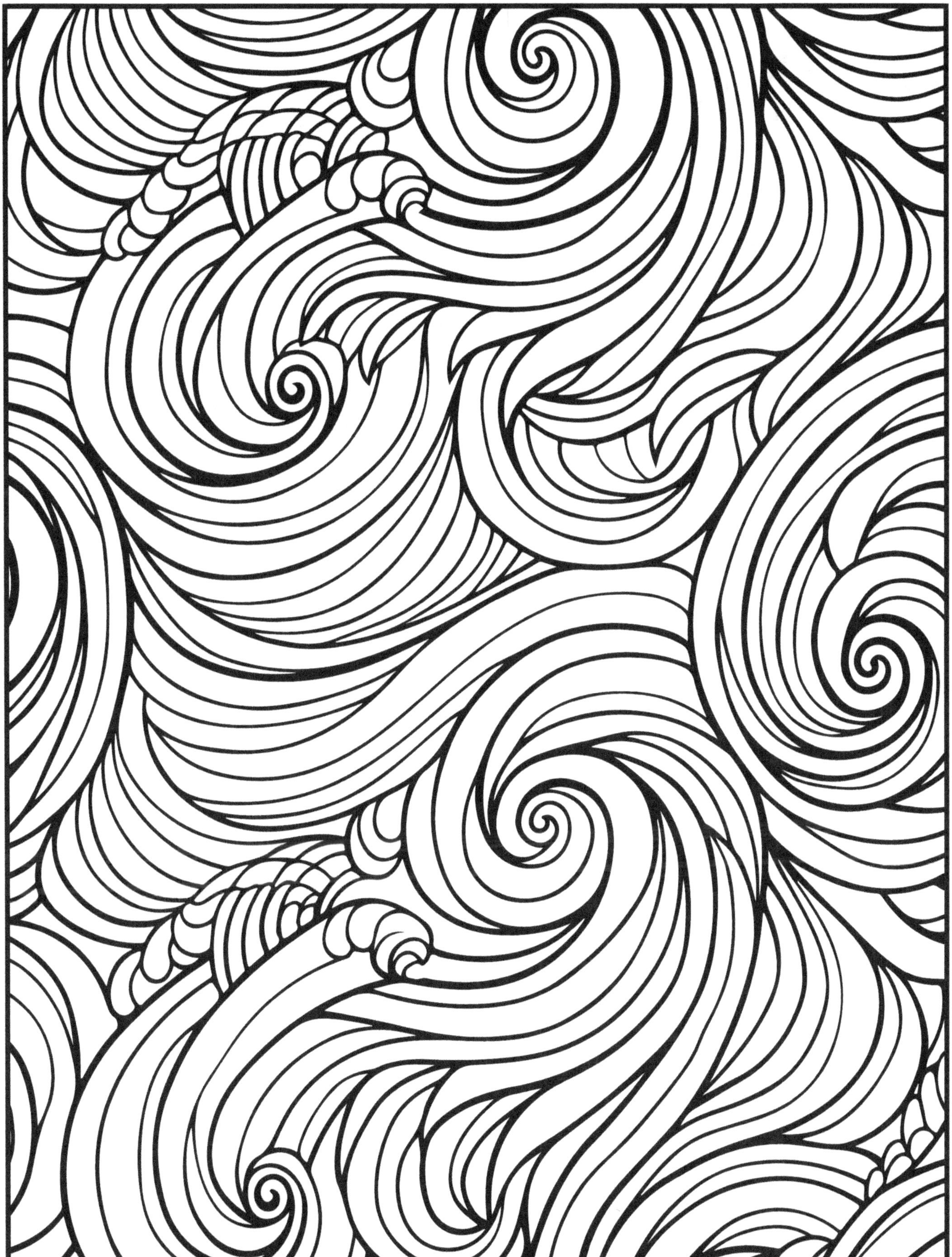

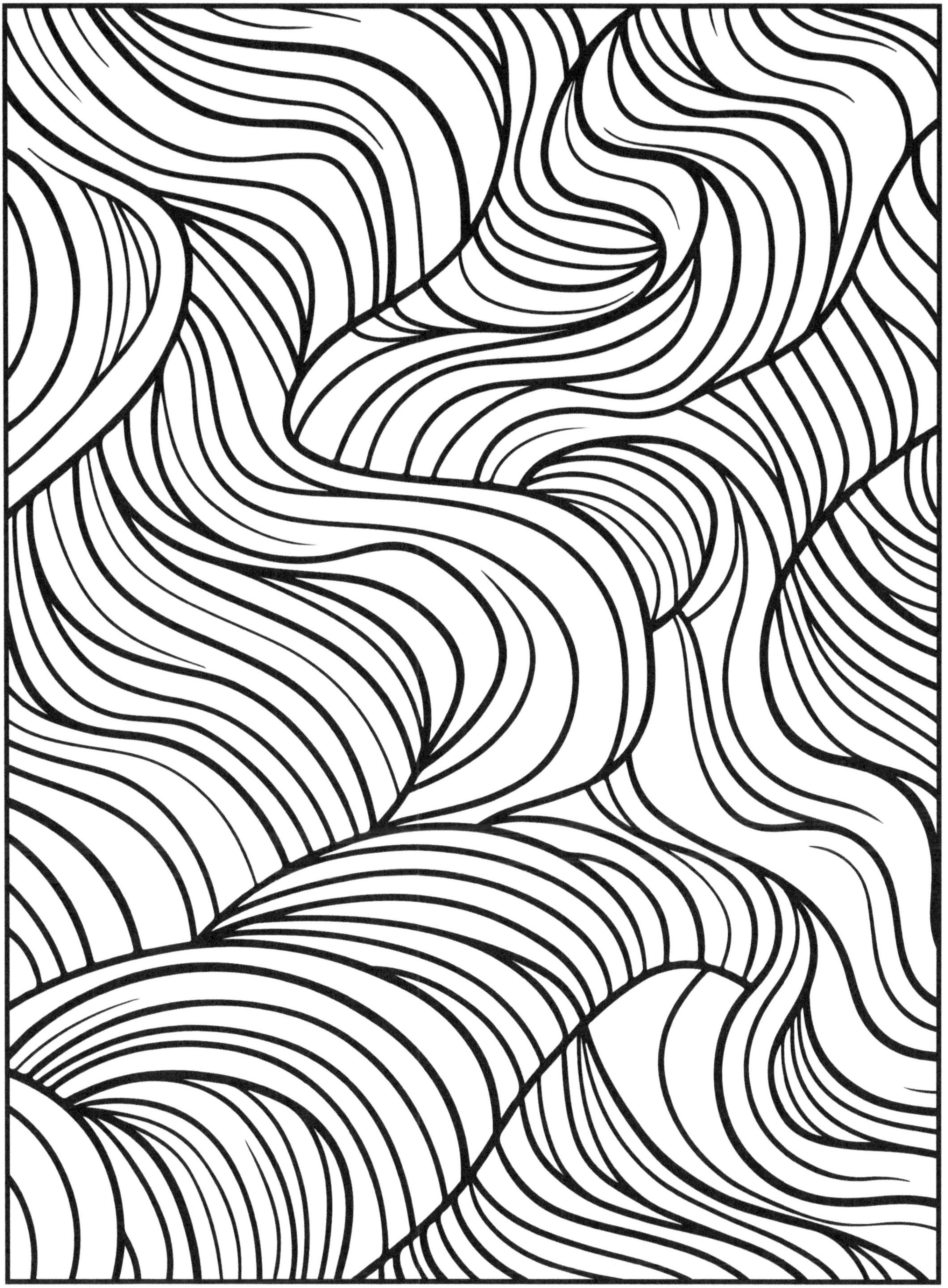

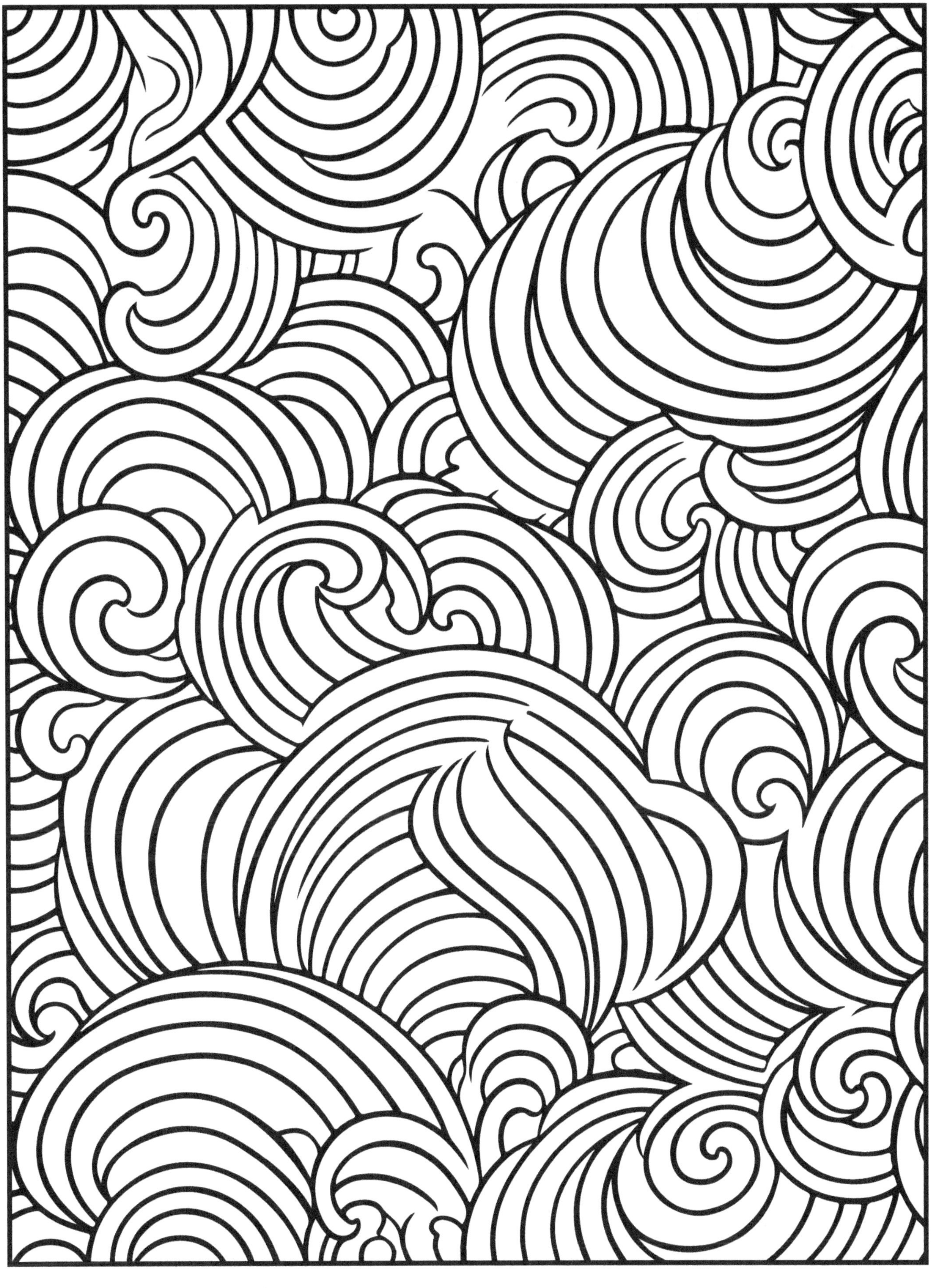

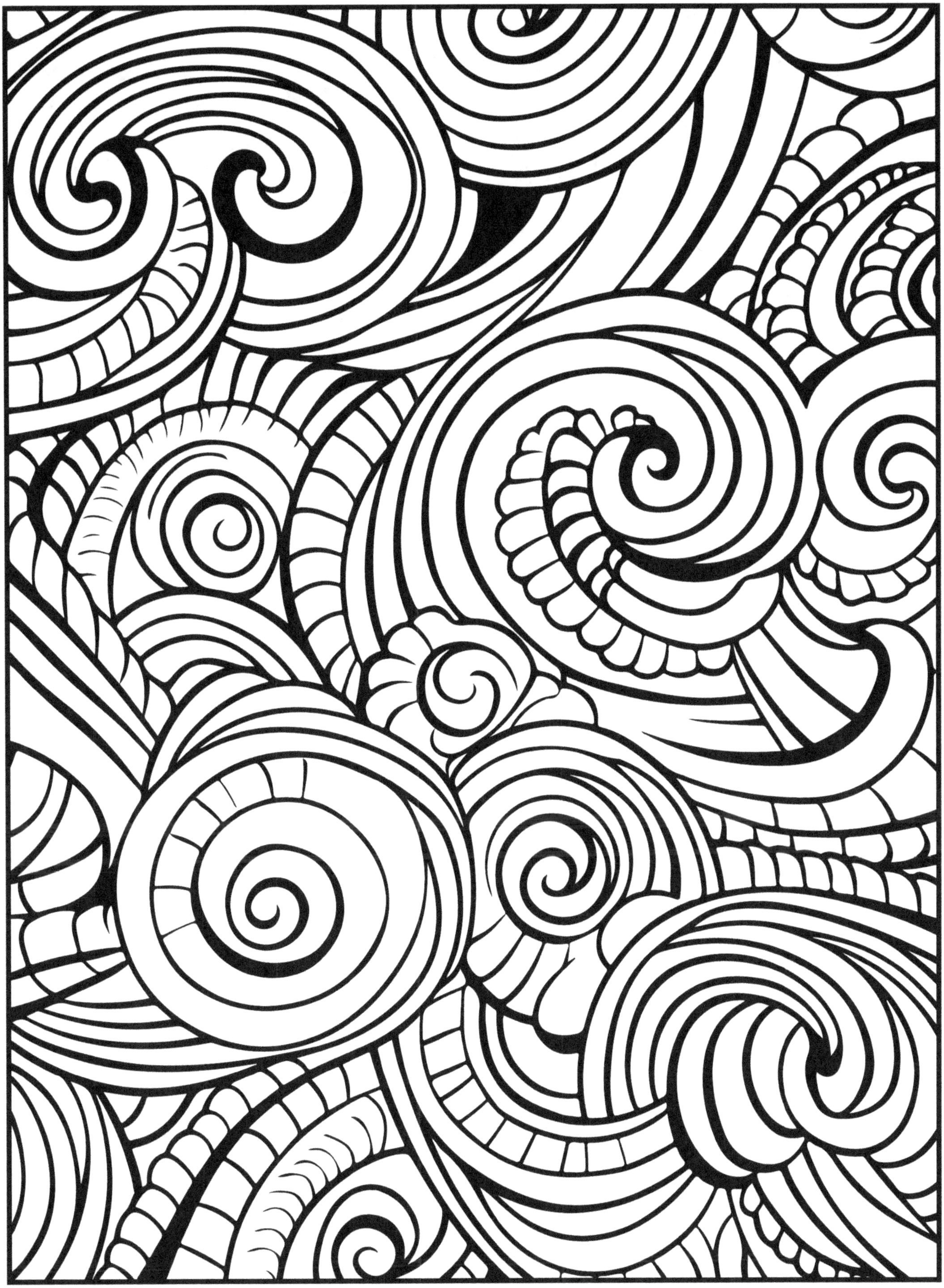

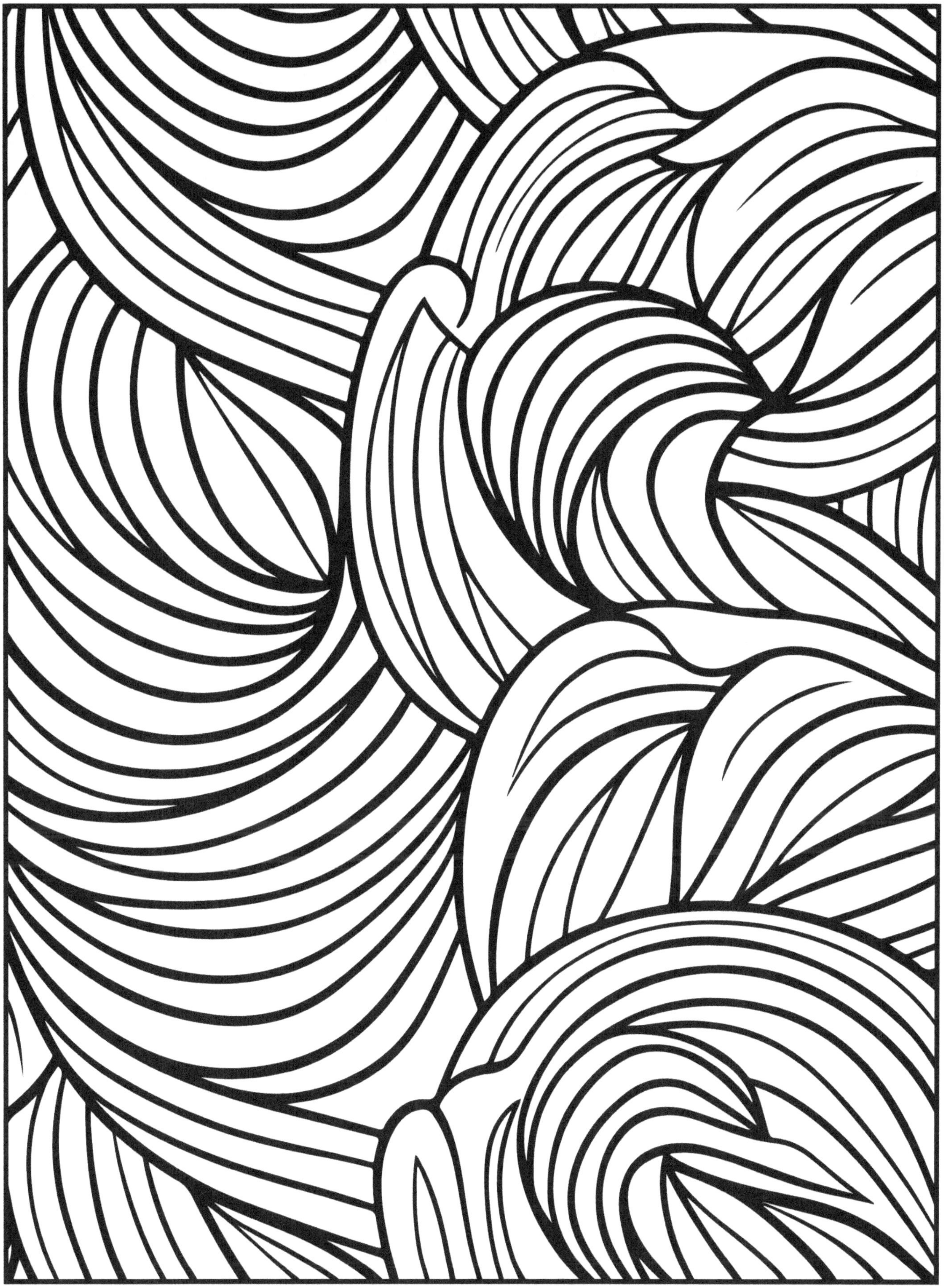

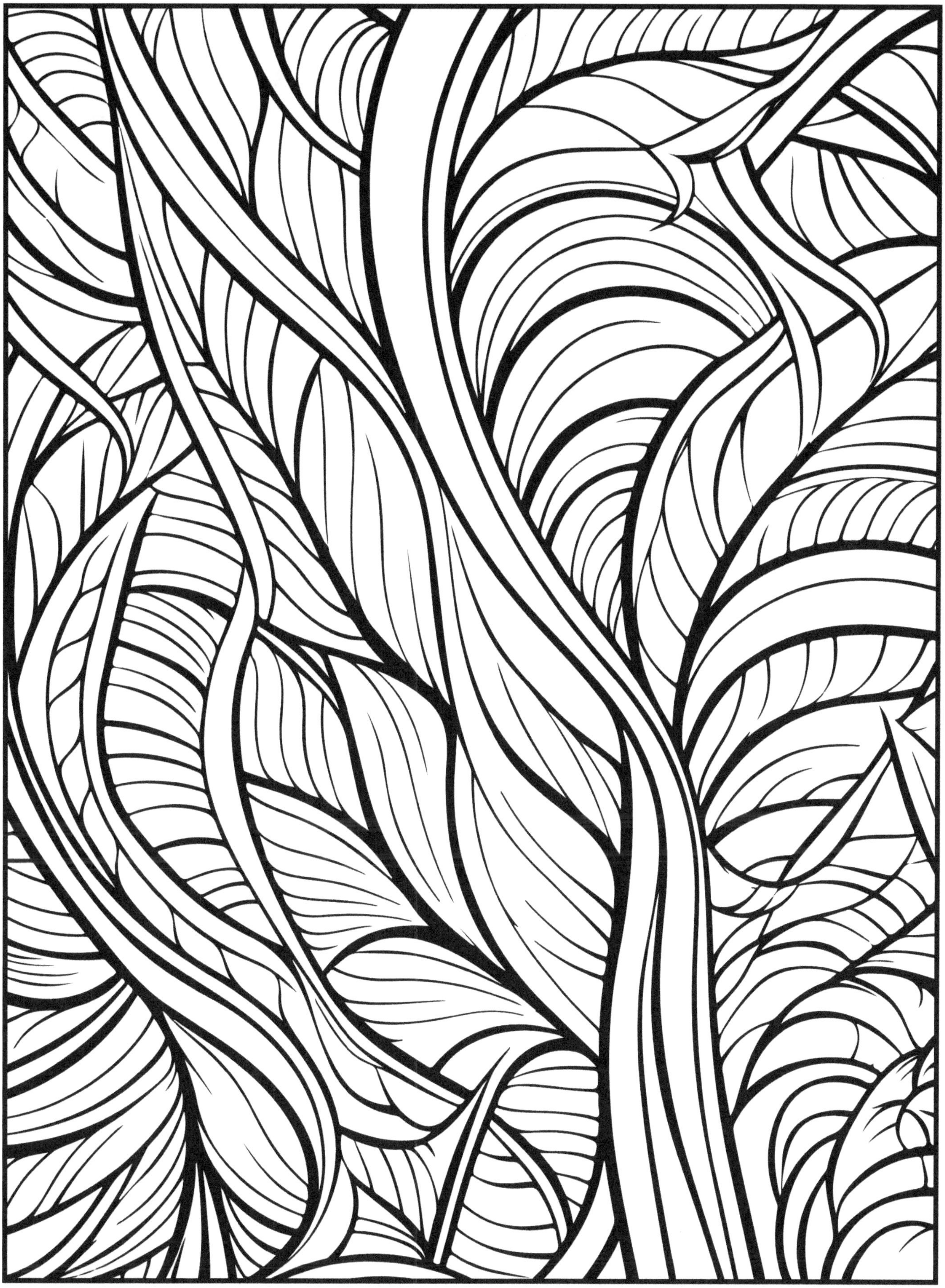

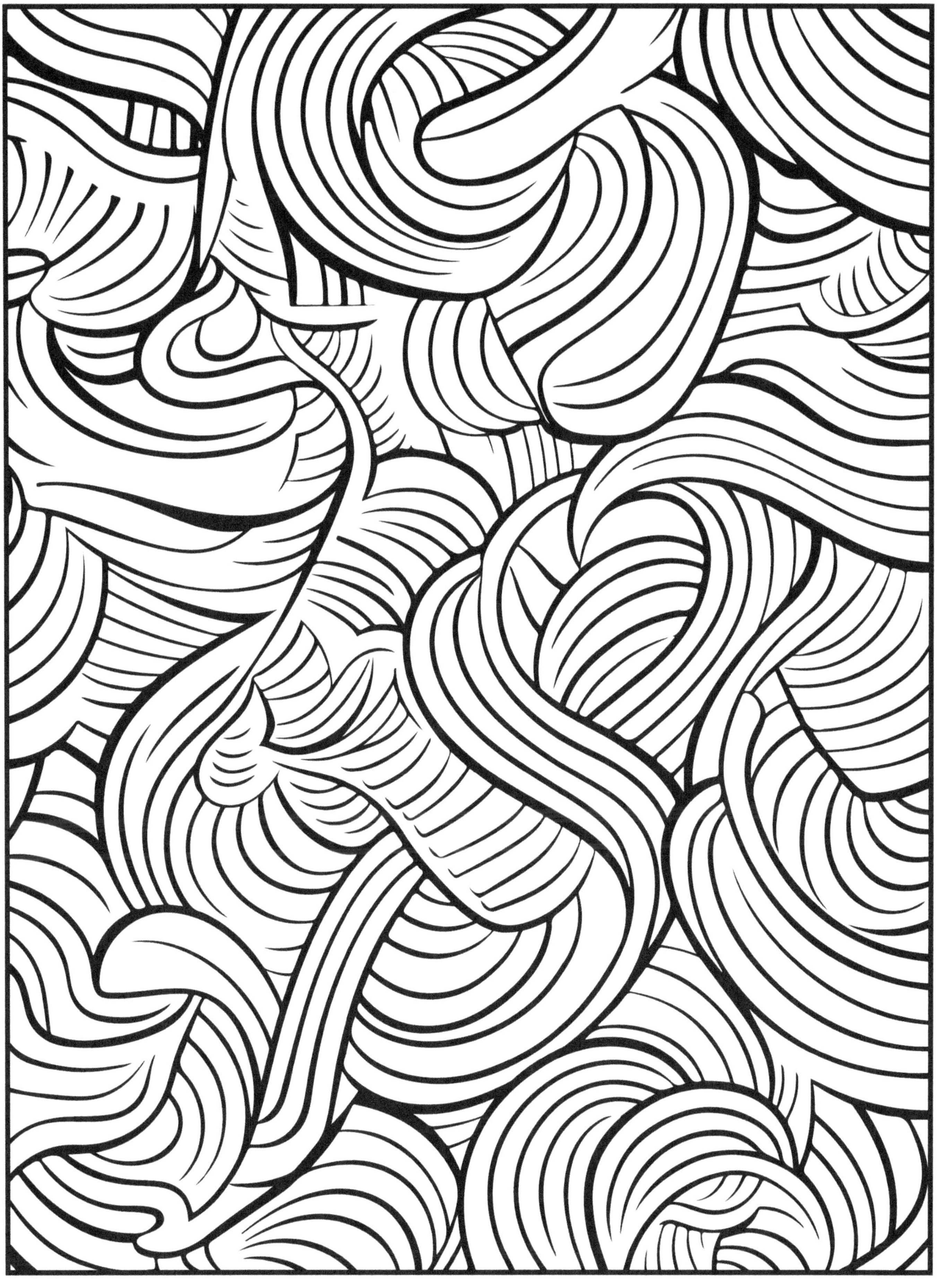

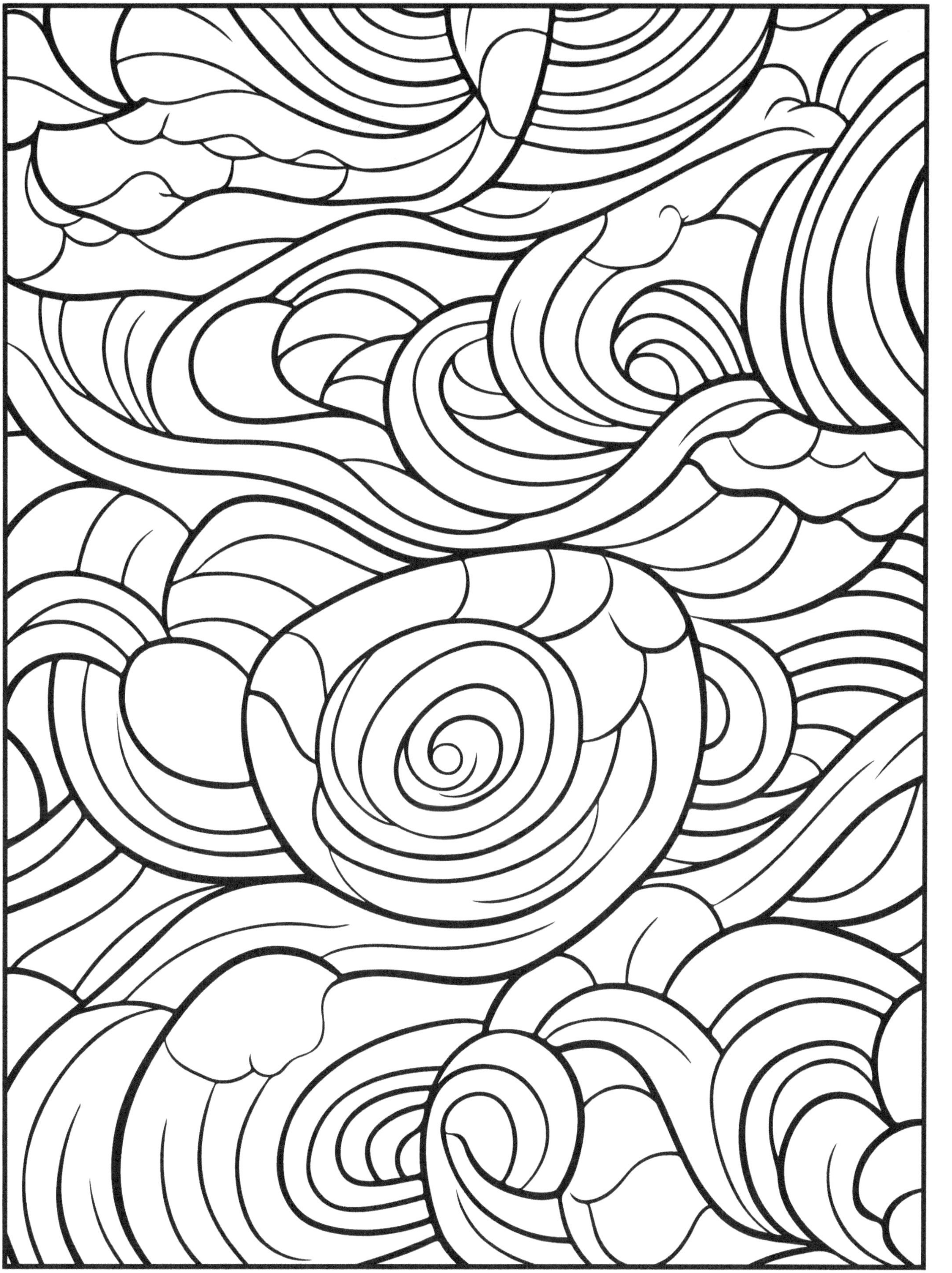

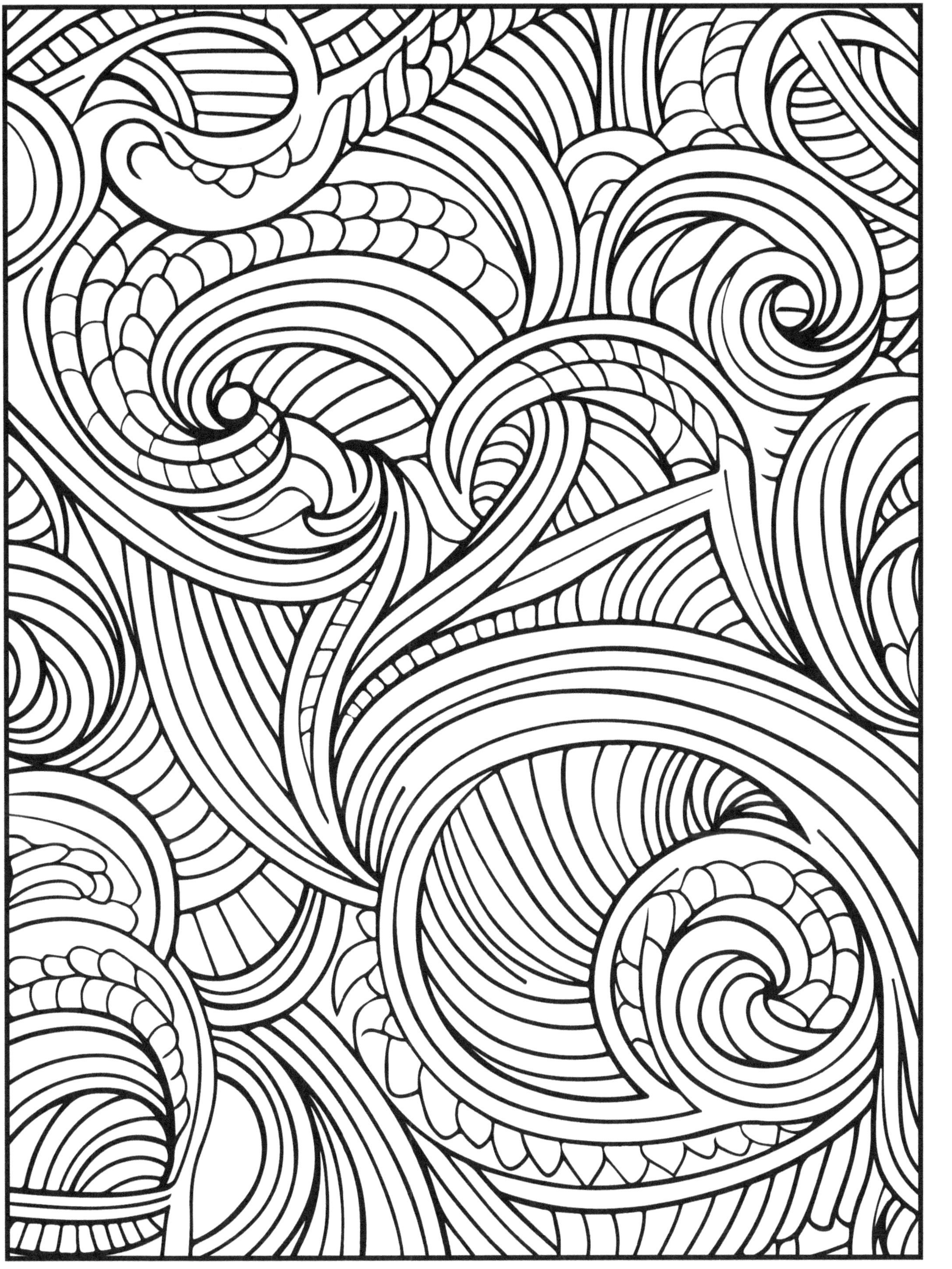

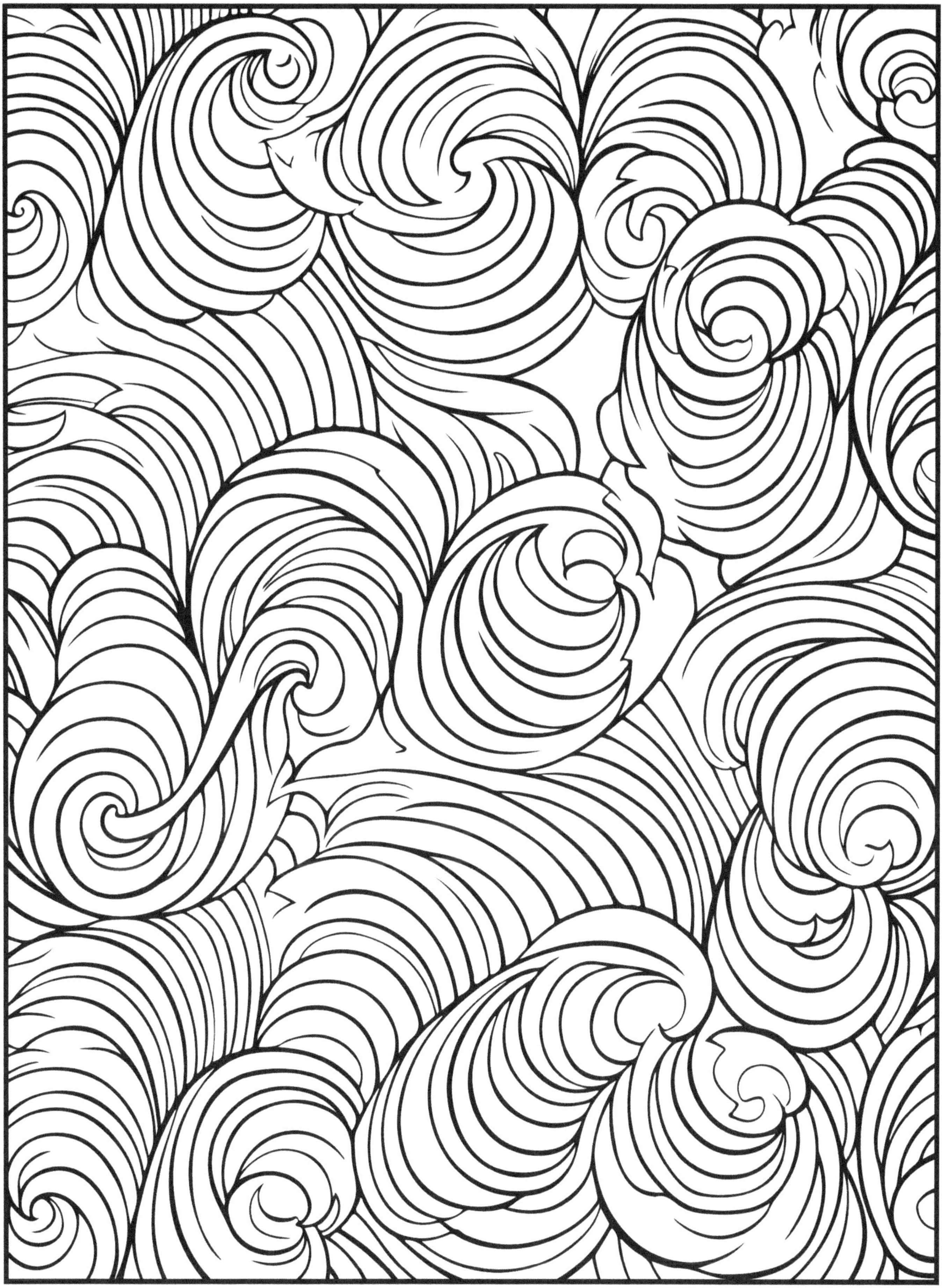

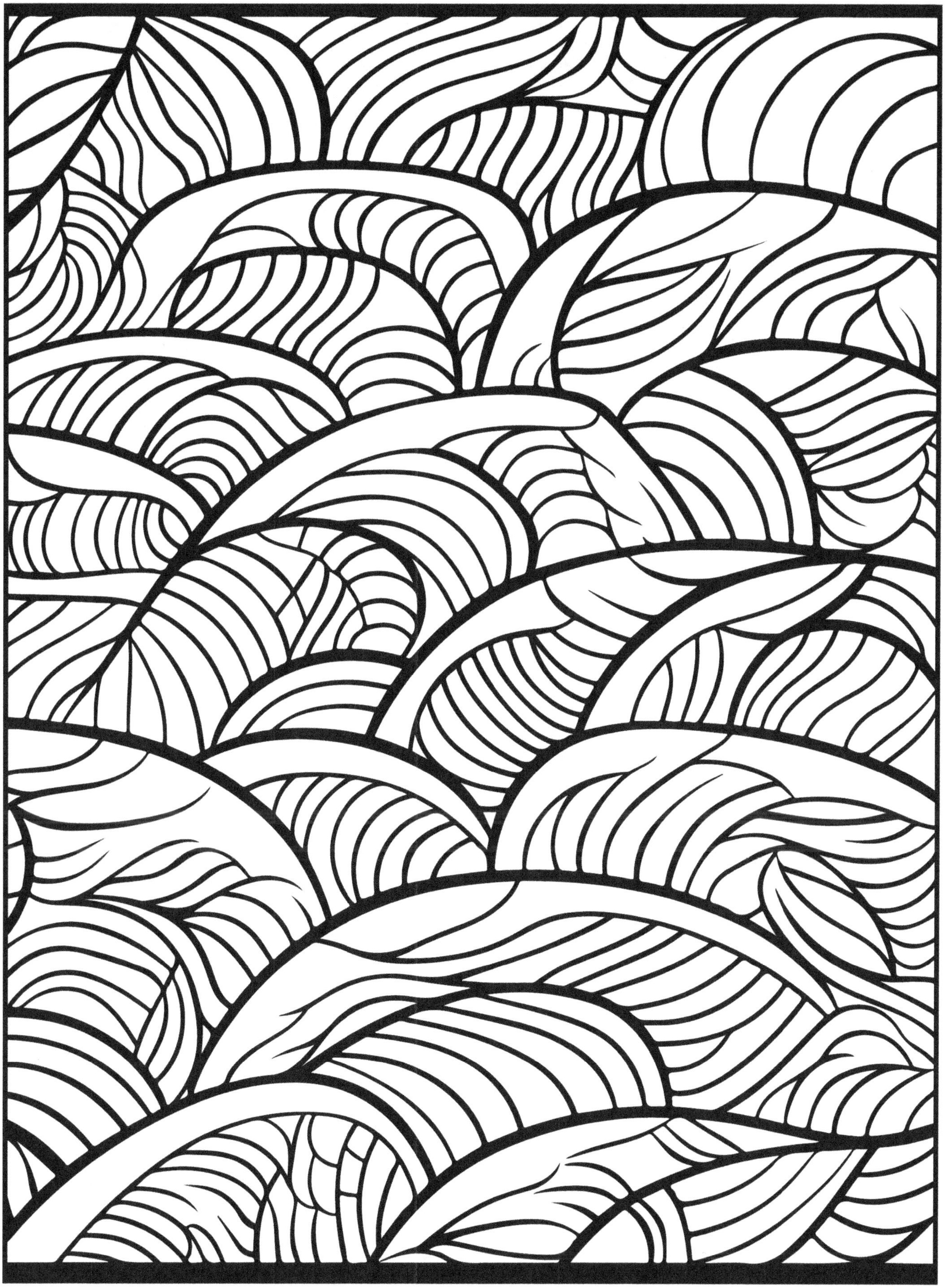

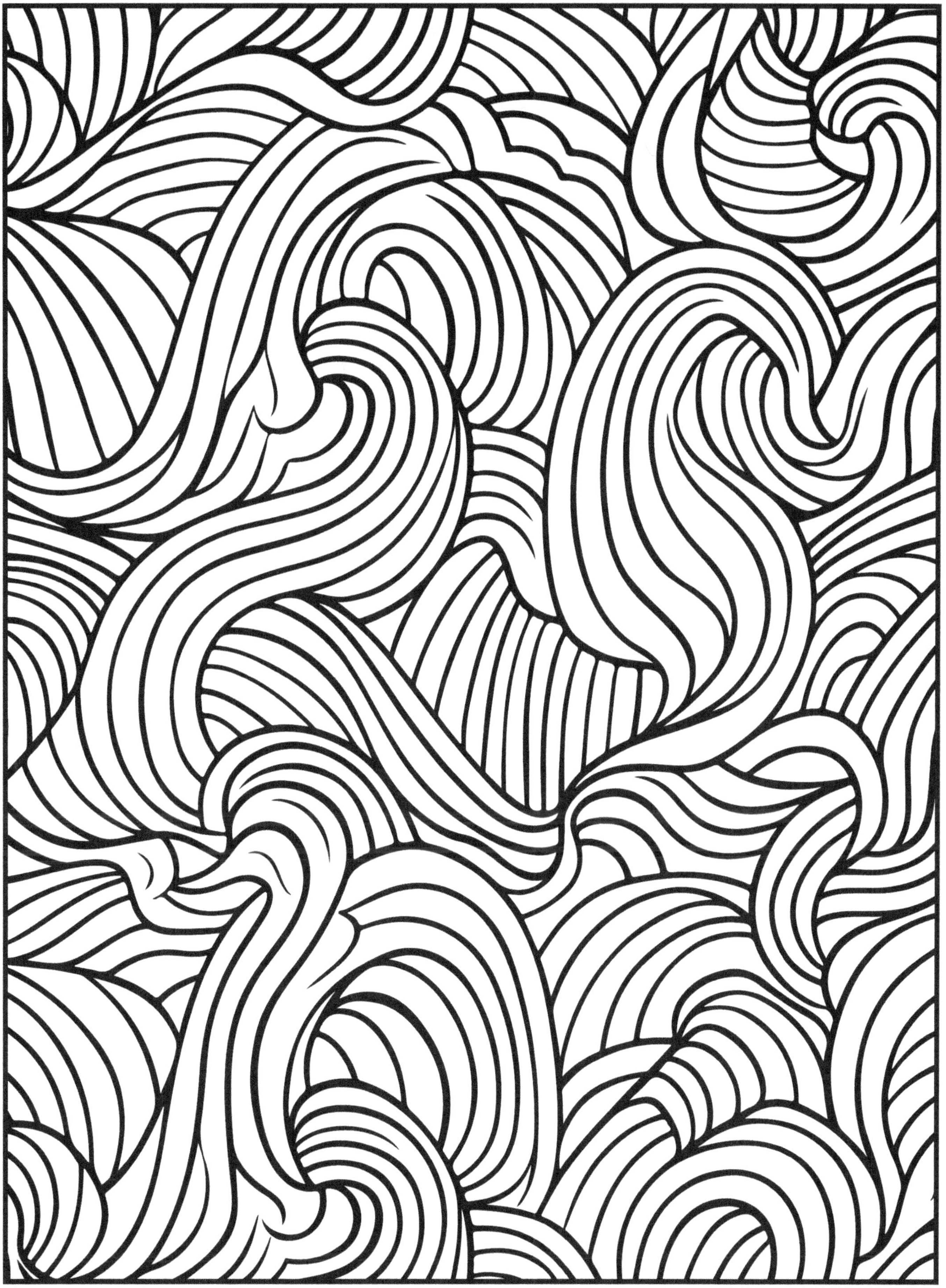

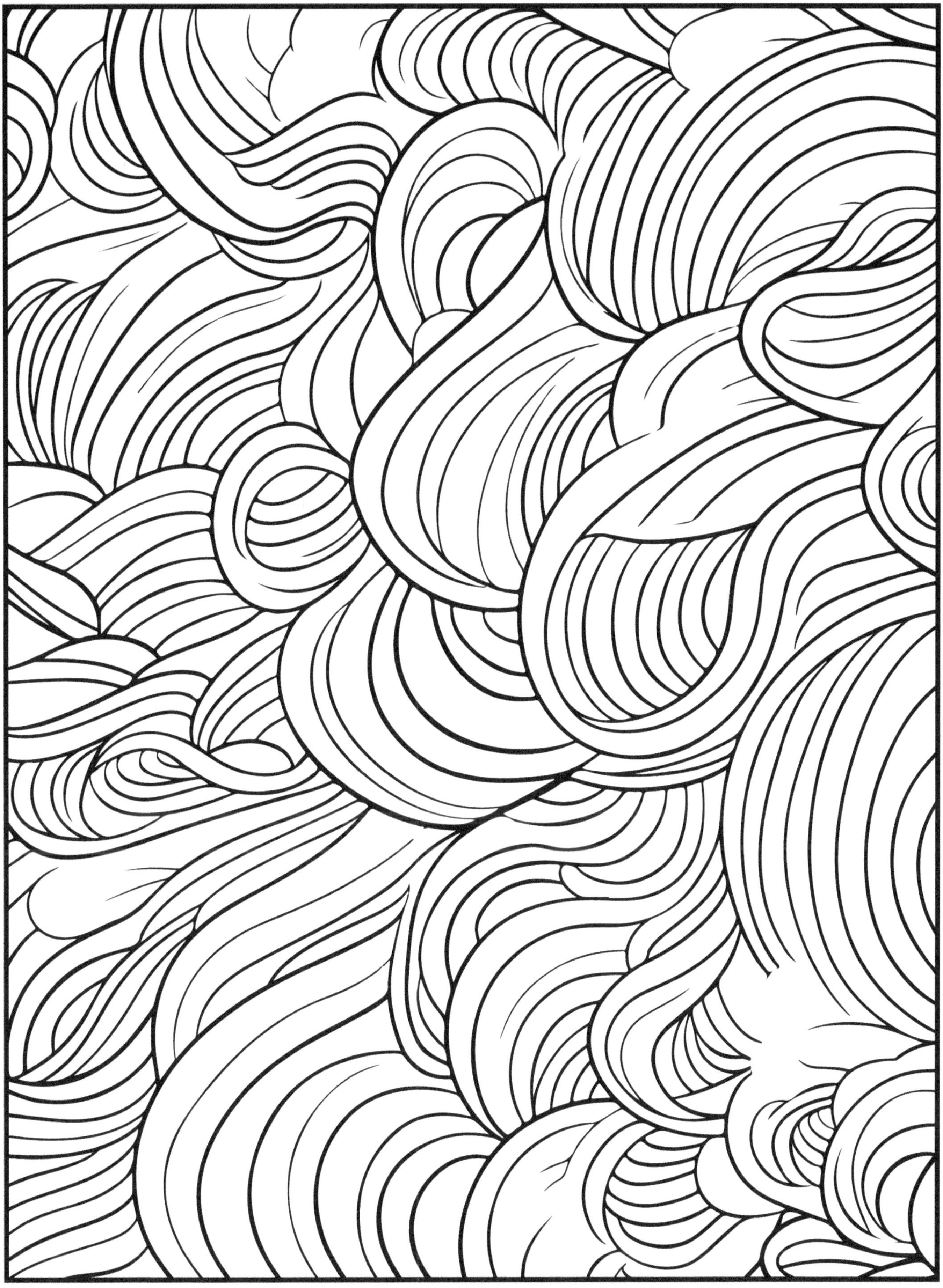

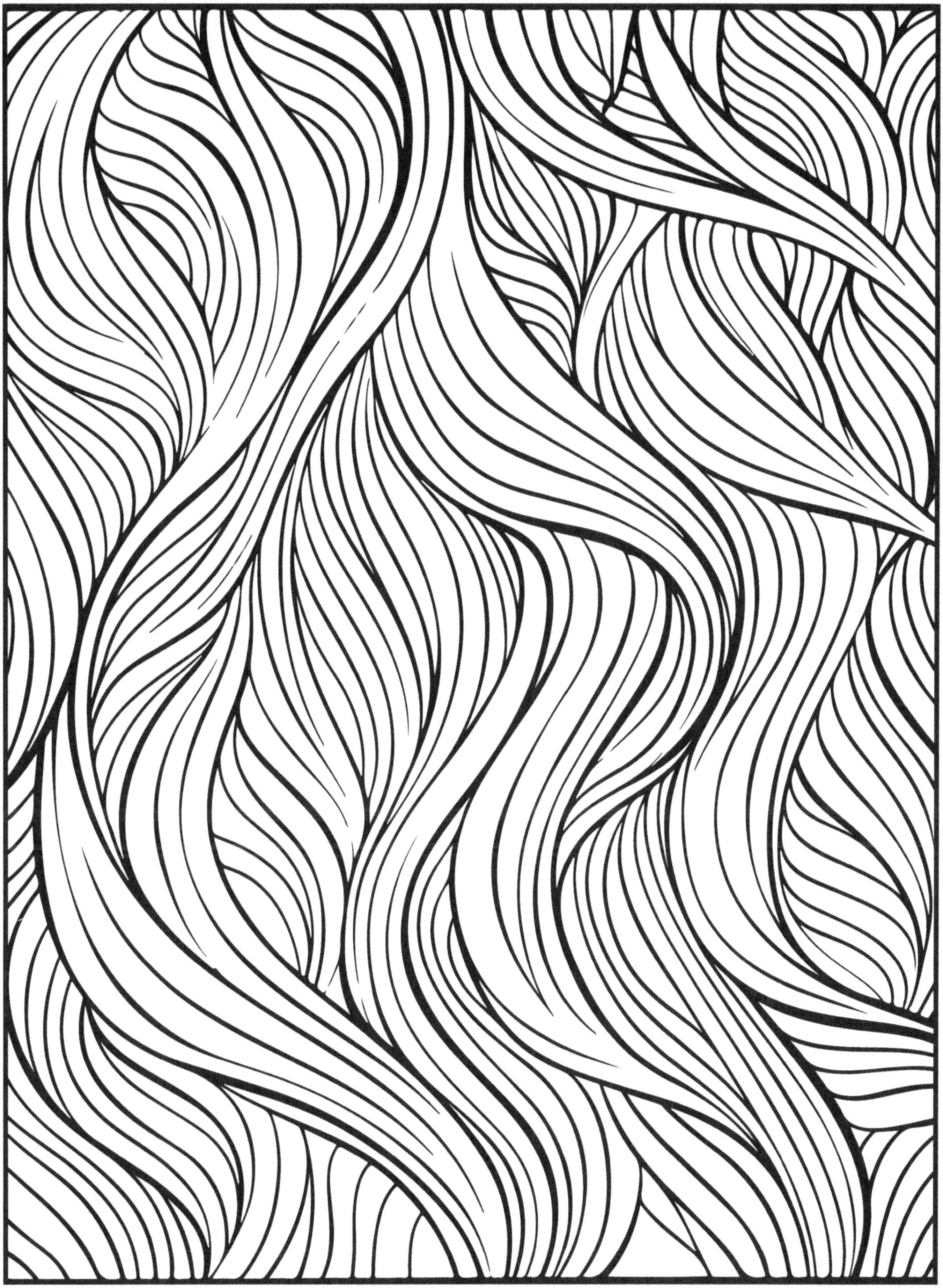

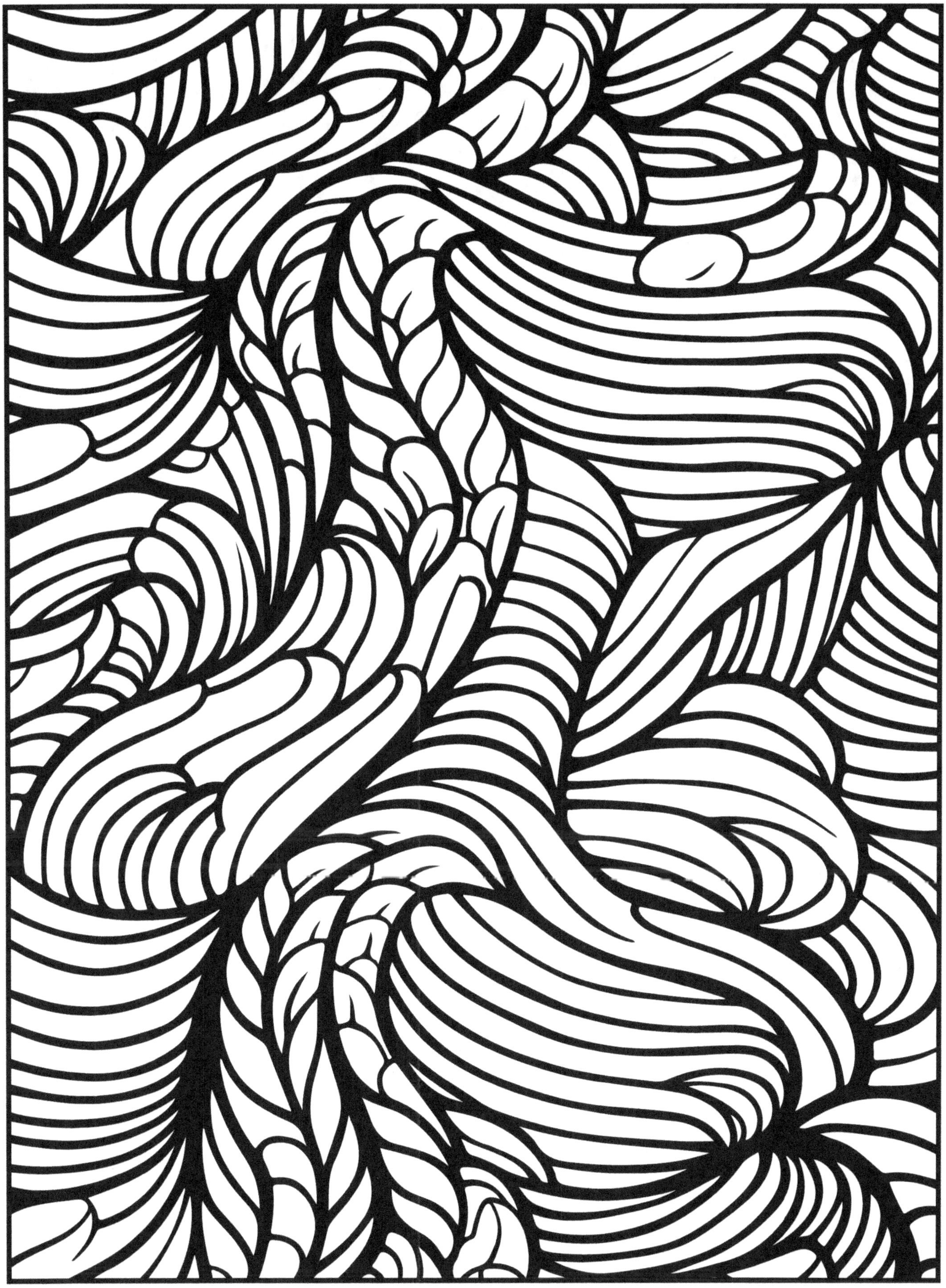

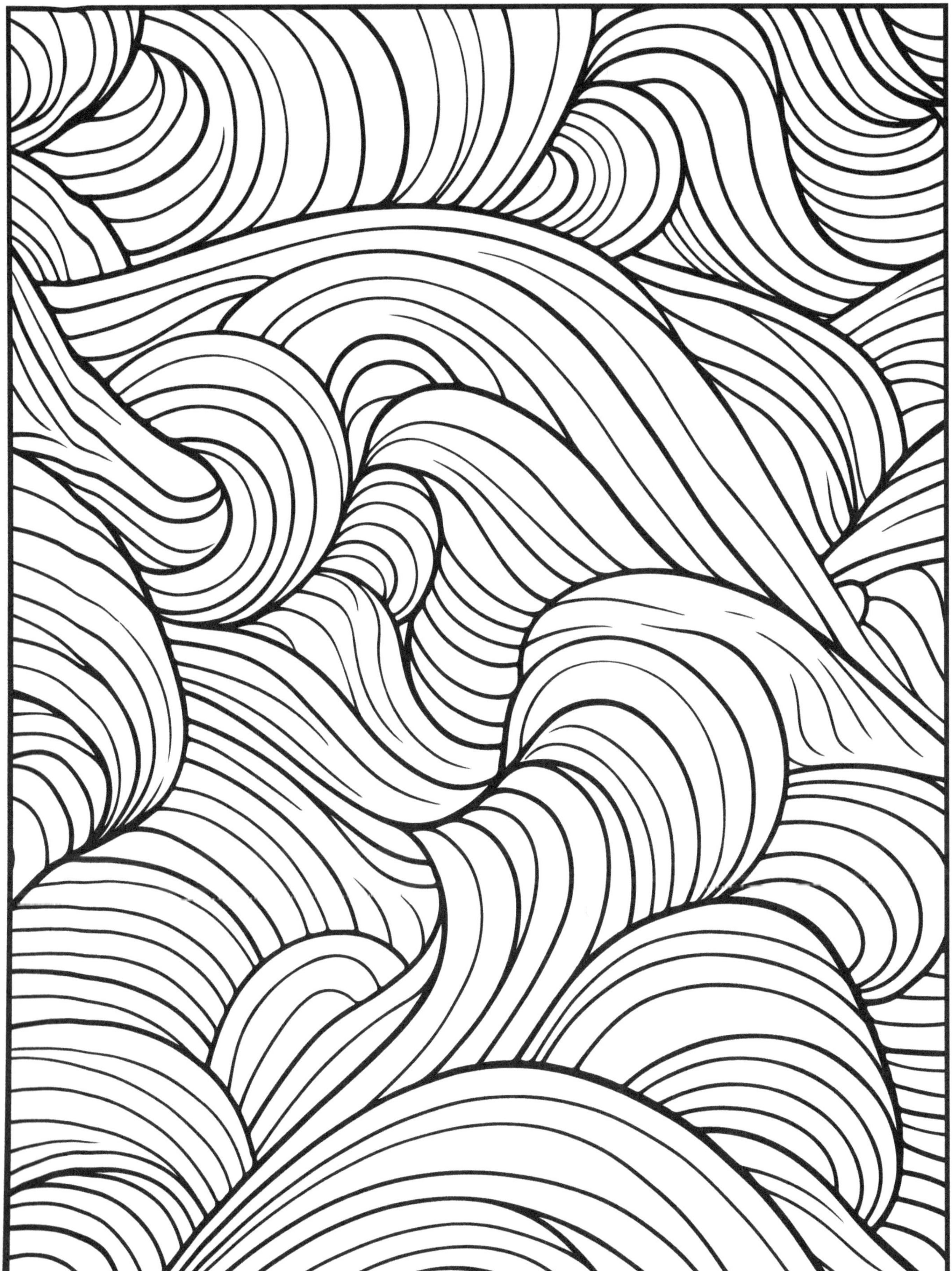

www.ingramcontent.com/pod-product-compliance
Lightning Source LLC
Chambersburg PA
CBHW082112220526
45472CB00009B/2147
* 9 7 9 8 3 2 7 8 3 9 0 0 7 *